Galdrastafir

A Collection of Icelandic Magical Staves

Matthew Leigh Embleton

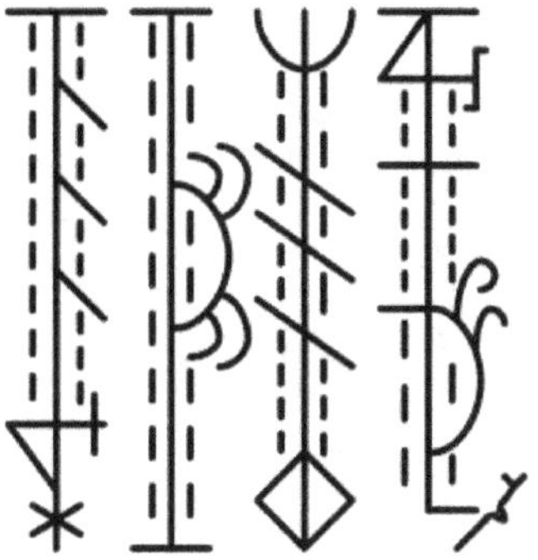

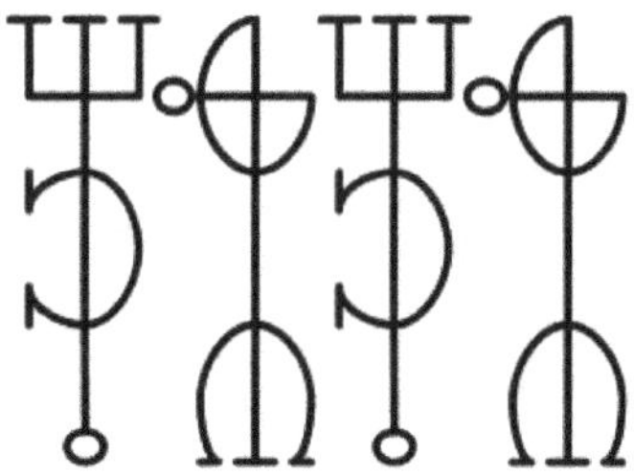

Copyright ©2020 Matthew Leigh Embleton. All rights reserved.

Galdrastafir

1. Origins and Evolution 1
2. Protection 4
3. Love 31
4. Luck 35
5. Healing 36
6. Enhancement 39
7. Setting Intentions 43
8. Sleep & Dreams 52
9. Fishing 57
10. Staves Against Theft 60
11. Legal 67
12. Influencing Behaviour 70
13. Concealment 75
14. Creating Fear in Enemies 77
15. Against Enemies 81
16. Miscellaneous 84
17. The Influence of Christianity 87

All images contained in this book are drawn by the author

Acknowledgments

I have long been fascinated by languages and history, and I am very grateful to the special people in my life who have supported and encouraged me in my work. Thank you for believing in me. You know who you are.

Introduction

In such times of increasing misunderstanding, incomplete information, misinformation, and misguided criticism, it has become necessary to add a number of clarifications in order to set the record straight in this expanded introduction.

The Viking Age and North Germanic Paganism

In recent decades popular culture has rediscovered the Viking Age and North Germanic Paganism with fresh eyes. From the pirates and sea raiders known as Vikings, to the fierce warriors called Berserkers, and the wider Norse or Nordic people as a whole, symbols played an important role in daily life and spirituality.

Today we find these symbols visually eye catching and their meanings fascinating. People all over the world are finding meaning in these symbols that resonate with their personality, identity, and spiritual beliefs.

Symbols for personal magic

These symbols are a representation of a thought or an idea, from a single line to an ever increasingly complex symmetry of lines, circles, intersecting lines, and bold striking angles. Perhaps one of the most popular of these symbols is the Vegvísir, one of the many Galdrastafir (praying or chanting staves) that appeared in Iceland after its settlement by Norse people in the late 9th century, but there are many many more.

Manuscript sources of Galdrastafir

The word 'manuscript' comes from the Medieval Latin '*manuscriptum*', which came from the Latin '*manu*' = by hand + '*scriptus*' = written. In the Norse tradition they are called '*handrit*' = hand written. The manuscripts that have survived contain a wealth of magical symbols drawn by hand in what were personal handbooks called '*galdrabók*' ('*galdra*' = spells, magic, or incantations + '*bók*' = book or '*bókir*' = books). Sometimes they are called a *grimoire* or *grimoires*, a term used restrospectively which is believed to be of Old French origin, referring to the tradition of manuscripts in Latin.

These *galdrabókir* were the result of collected and shared knowledge within a community of practitioners of magic, often in secrecy. For a while it was illegal to own such a book, and so they were kept hidden and remained for the personal use of the owner in their personal collection. They may well have been used as a reference to teach the tradition to initiates, but the idea that in their written form they were designed to be purely instructional on their own and read like a catalogue without any guidance by an elder is a false one.

As anyone who like myself has trawled through these manuscripts will tell you, in some cases there are accompanying sentences explaining the meaning and instruction on the use of each symbol, and in many cases the very name of the symbol told the owner all they needed to know.

From the name or title of the symbol, how that symbol was used was a matter of personal choice, depending on the circumstances and the type of incantation or spell that was to be performed. This use would have been guided by the person's own understanding of the nature and the spirit of magic, of signalling their intentions to the universe.

A single symbol in a *galdrabók* is called a '*galdrastafr*' = galdra or galdor stave. The plural is *galdrastafir*, therefore the plural term 'galdrastafirs' with the plural -s suffix is incorrect, as the term *galdrastafir* is already plural.

The misuse of symbols

Galdrastafir have been associated with the misuse of runes and Norse symbols as a whole. In 2019 reports emerged claiming that depictions of runes and Norse symbols, including those represented in traditional Viking jewellery, may soon be banned in Sweden, including *Mjolnir* (Thor's Hammer), the *Valknut*, and the *Vegvísir* ('way-seer' / 'way marker' / Nordic compass).

For the last 120 years, runes and other Norse symbols have been misguidedly misused, misrepresented, and misinterpreted by some, as part of systems of propaganda for extreme and objectionable political agendas. This form of cultural appropriation has done great damage in obscuring and twisting the original and true meanings of the runes.

The misuse of runes by the Nazis is well documented and well known, but sadly this knowledge is sometimes inadvertently misused by people who in their noble fight against objectionable political ideas and their association with historical atrocities end up losing their way, equating this misuse of runes and Norse symbols with that of a 2,000 year old tradition in the case of runes, and a approximately 1,000 year old tradition in the case of Galdrastafir, which is experienced innocently by pagans and spiritualists around the world, who have been mistakenly and undeservedly reviled as being associated with ideas and beliefs that they do not have and find abhorrent as much as the next person.

There are anecdotal accounts in discussion forums on the internet describing how people have punitively snatched such pendants from around the necks of wearers exclaiming "Nazis wear these!"... to which the correct answer must be... "*...and so do millions of innocent pagans!*".

Hate symbols

The Anti-Defamation League has an online database of hate symbols containing runes misused by Nazis and far-right groups, rightly stating that because these runes and Norse symbols continue "to be used by non-racists, typically adherents of neo-pagan religions, one should not simply assume that a particular use of this symbol is racist, but should carefully judge it in its context".

Conclusion

By discovering these magical symbols, you are rightly reaffirming the true meaning of their culture. Not only that but in true spirit you are refusing to allow access to this culture to be denied to you by those who mistakenly believe that the misuse of these symbols is their only use. Such people seeking to revile and punish innocent users of pagan symbols are actually enabling far right organisations to steal this culture.

The magic of the Norse people worked because they believed that it worked. They believed in the process of signalling and communicating their intentions and desirable outcomes to the forces around them, projecting them into the universe, and having the confidence and belief to make things happen.

1. Origins and Evolution

The Icelandic word 'galdra' comes from the Old Norse word '*galdr*' meaning the practice of magic or '*seiðr*' by the singing or chanting of spells or incantations.

The Icelandic word 'stafur' (plural 'stafir') comes from the Old Norse word '*stafr*' meaning a letter or symbol, or a staff or stick, in this case with magical meaning and purpose.

These galdrastafir are preserved in a number of manuscripts and grimoires dating as far back as the late Middle Ages, often in the form of collections, compendiums, or 'recipe books' of magic, such as the following:

> AM 434 a 12mo (Lækningakver, Iceland, 1475-1525)
> ATA Amb 2 F 16-26(Isländksa Svartkonstboken, 1550-1650)
> ÍB 383 4to (Huld, Iceland, 1860)
> LBS 143 8vo (Galdrakver, Iceland, 1670)
> LBS 2413 8vo (Rúna-og Galdrakver, Iceland)
> LBS 2917a 4to (Galdrakver, Iceland)
> LBS 4375 8vo (Galdrastafir, Iceland, 1900-1949)
> LBS 4627 8vo (Galdrakver, Iceland)
> LBS 4689 8vo (Galdrakver, Iceland)
> LBS 764 8vo (Galdrakver, Iceland, 1780)
> LBS 977 4to (Samtíningur, Iceland, 1818-1820)

Galdra and the practice of magic or '*seiðr*' in general are mentioned in Norse Literature in several different texts:

Eddic Poems
> Grógaldr (The Spell of Gróa)
> Hávamál (Sayings of the High One)
> Oddrúnargrátr (Oddrún's lament or Oddrún's Poem)
> Skírnismál (The Lay of Skírnir)

Legendary Sagas
> Bósa saga ok Herrauðs (The Saga of Bósi and Herraud)
> Friðþjófs saga hins frœkna (Frithiof's Saga)
> Ynglinga saga (The Saga of the Yngling Family)

Icelandic Sagas
> Eiríks saga rauða (The Saga of Eric the Red)
> Vatnsdæla saga (The Saga of the People of Vatnsdalur)

These texts give the reader a glimpse into the importance of magic and those who practiced it in Norse society.

The Norse god Óðinn or Odin is strongly associated with the magical tradition, including his self-sacrifice in search of knowledge of runes and magic.

Galdrastafir 1. Origins and Evolution

Some galdrastafir, particularly those that employ symmetry into their design show a resemblance and possible evolution from the formation and use of bindrunes, taking a rune that contains a value or significance, and then replicating it over several points of symmetry.

The simplest of runes is perhaps the 'Isaz' rune, a simple straight line related to the letter 'I' meaning ice, being in a frozen state, or binding, is used to bind several runes together into a single symbol or grapheme. Here by example is the Isaz rune combined and overlapped with increasing points of symmetry.

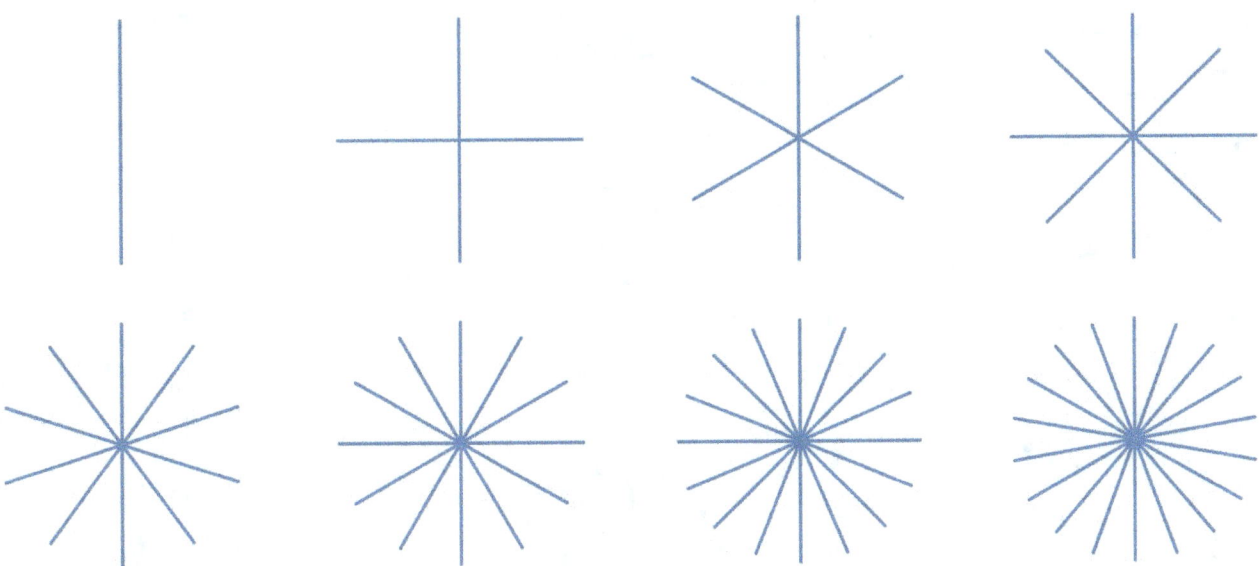

The 'Ansuz' rune (ᚠ) represents divine speech, wisdom, source, connection, and communication.

Here is the Ansuz rune employed in the same way as above.

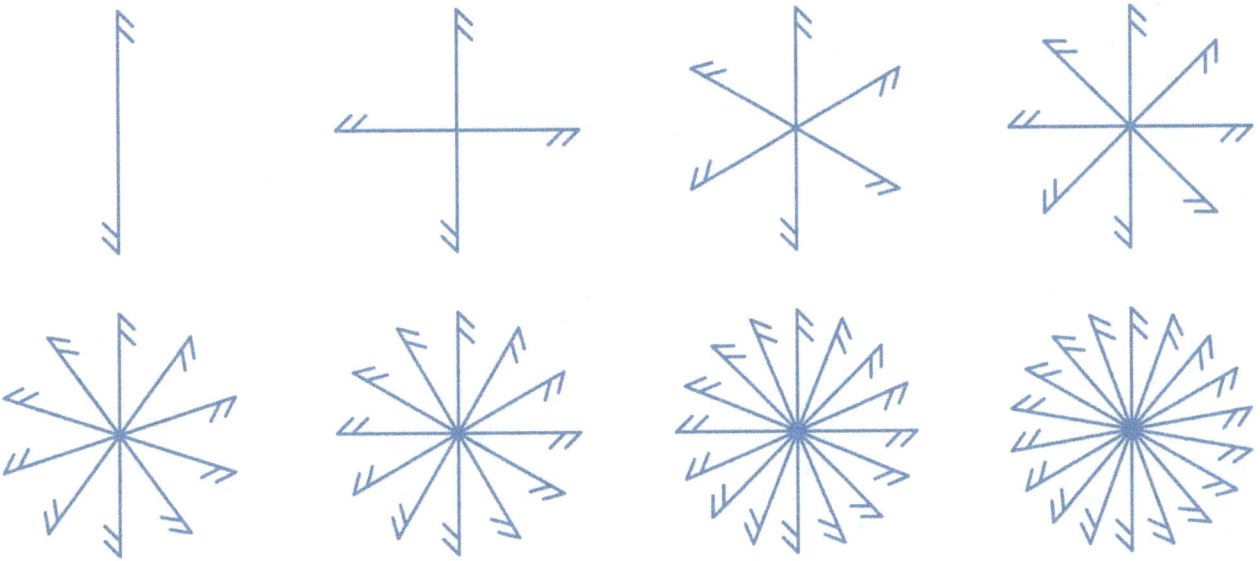

The reader will see many staves in this book that follow this pattern of formulation, with modified characters across the symmetric points of the stave.

Galdrastafir   1. Origins and Evolution

There are a series of common elements of the design of Galdrastafir which are described as 'modifiers'.

Because of the frequency of their occurrence, there are varied yet inconclusive theories on each of their special purposes or functions, such as energy flowing in and out of the stave, being amplified etc., or even invoking gods from the Norse pantheon.

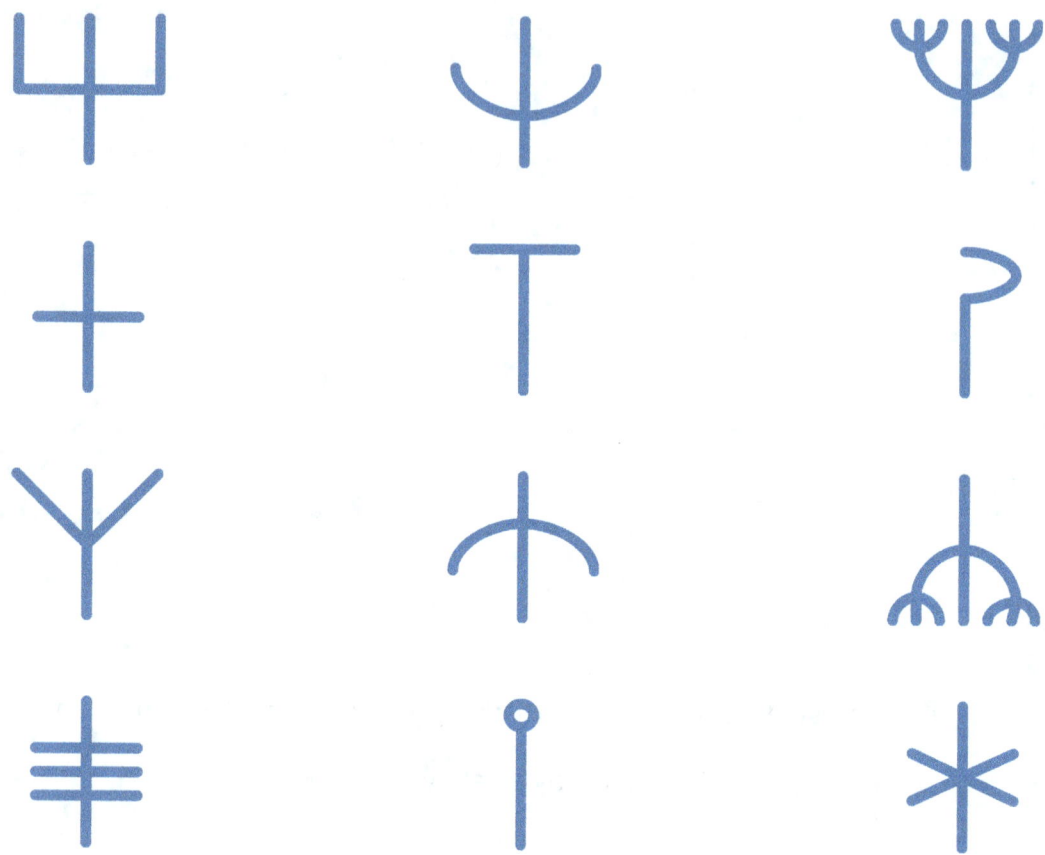

2. Protection

Against All Witchery

Have this sign in your right hand against all fear of witchery.

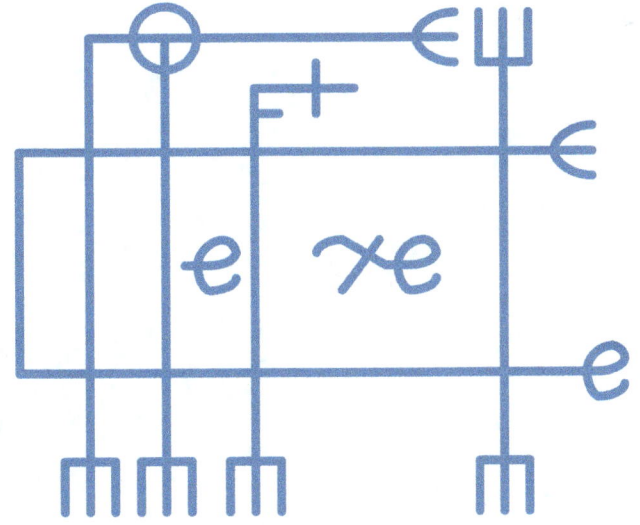

Against Foreboding When You Go Into Darkness

Carve this sign on rice-oak (hríseik) and wear it under your left arm.

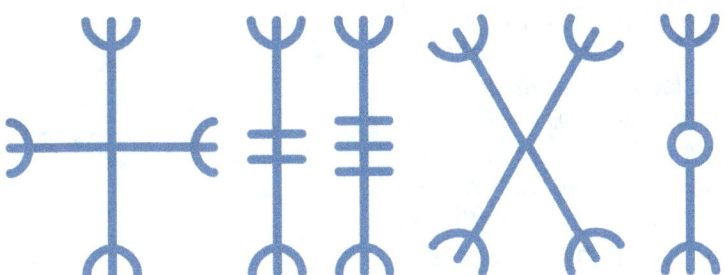

Galdrastafir   *2. Protection*

Brynja
(Byrnie)
LBS 4375 8vo 0023v 03

Carve on cedarwood and colour with blood from your right breast, and you will never freeze to death.

Fengr
(Against Stefnivargar, Both Foxes and Mice)
LBS 4375 8vo 0009v 01

A stefnivarg is an animal that has been given power by magic and then sent to do harm to someone.

Carve this stave with blood on fox pelt, and walk clockwise and anticlockwise over the hills and high verges of your farmland. Recite spells and invocations until all the noxious creatures have been gathered together. Then bind them and kill them.

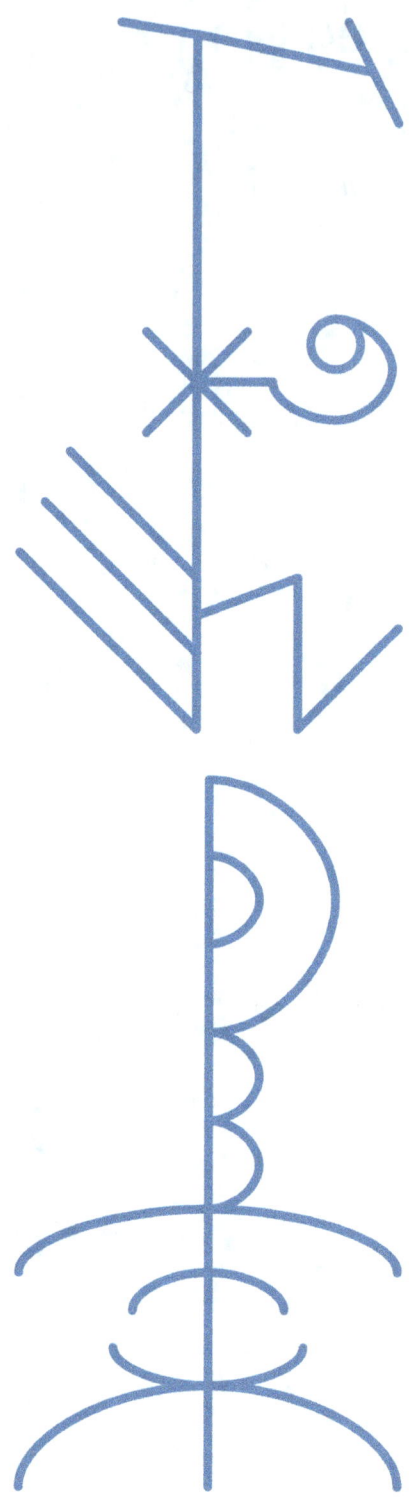

Fjárvarnarstafur
(Protective Stave For Sheep)
LBS 4375 8vo 0002v 03

To prevent the place where your sheep are grazing from being flooded, carve this stave into the horn of the eldest wether (a castrated ram).

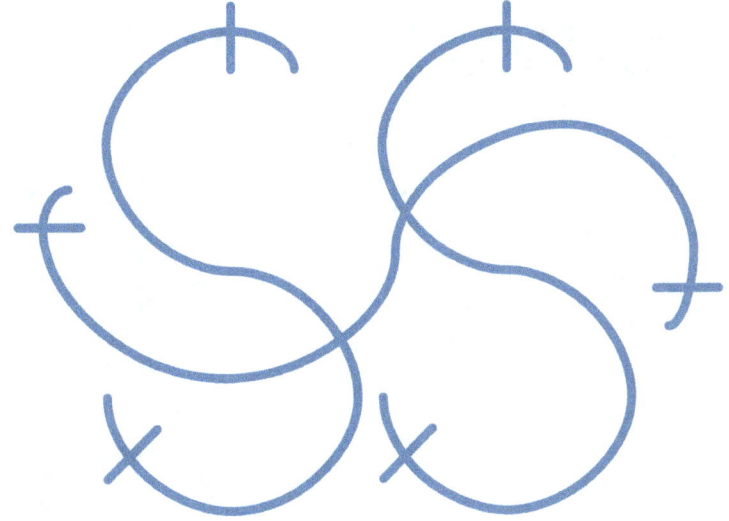

Fjölnir
(Against Stefnivargar, Both Foxes and Mice)
LBS 4375 8vo 0009v 05

A stefnivarg is an animal that has been given power by magic and then sent to do harm to someone.

Carve this stave with blood on fox pelt, and walk clockwise and anticlockwise over the hills and high verges of your farmland. Recite spells and invocations until all the noxious creatures have been gathered together. Then bind them and kill them.

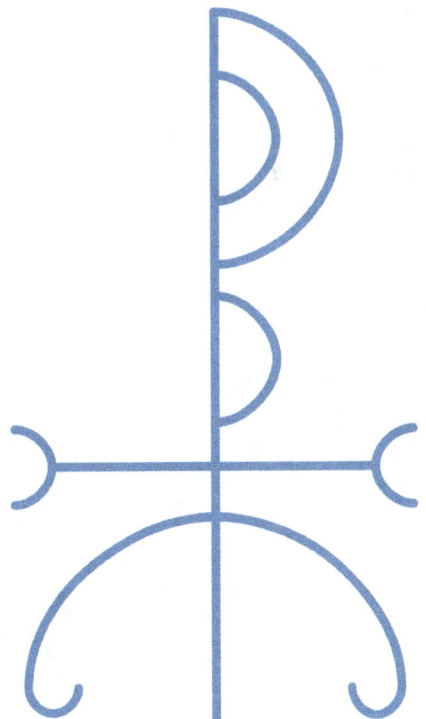

Galdrastafir 2. Protection

**Fransskriftarstafur 1
(French-Script Stave Against
Hatred and Evil Thoughts 1)**

Carve on oak and colour with blood from your nasal septum, and then wear it on the crown of your head.

**Fransskriftarstafur 2
(French-Script Stave Against
Hatred and Evil Thoughts 2)**

Carve on oak and colour with blood from your nasal septum, and then wear it on the crown of your head.

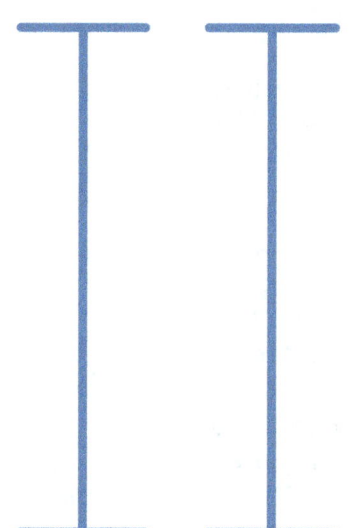

Fransskriftarstafur 3
(French-Script Stave Against Hatred and Evil Thoughts 3)

Carve on oak and colour with blood from your nasal septum, and then wear it on the crown of your head.

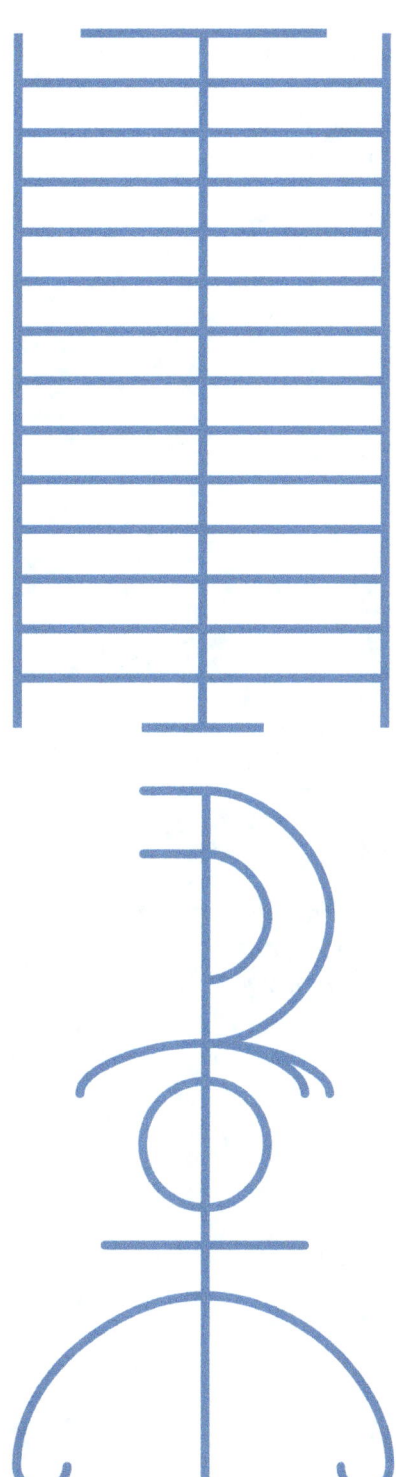

Freyr
(Against Stefnivargar, Both Foxes and Mice)
LBS 4375 8vo 0009v 04

A stefnivarg is an animal that has been given power by magic and then sent to do harm to someone.

Carve this stave with blood on fox pelt, and walk clockwise and anticlockwise over the hills and high verges of your farmland. Recite spells and invocations until all the noxious creatures have been gathered together. Then bind them and kill them.

Galdrastafir   2. Protection

Herzlustafir
(Strengthening Staves)
IB 383 4to 0027r 01
LBS 2917a 4to 0015v 02
LBS 4627 8vo 0014r 01

Wear this on your left breast to strengthen your courage.

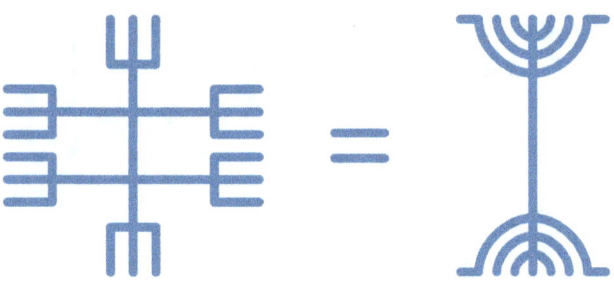

Hjálmur
(Helm)
LBS 4375 8vo 0023v 04

Inscribe on lignite (jet stone) and colour with blood from your nose and you will never go insane.

Innsigli Salomons 1
(Seal Of Solomon 1)
IB 383 4to 0025v 01
LBS 2917a 4to 0013r 01

This one is carried for protection.

Innsigli Salomons 2
(Seal Of Solomon 2)
LBS 2917a 4to 0018v 01
LBS 764 8vo 0007v 01

Protective stave against ice buildup and lack of pasturage. Works best from the start of Þorri (mid January to mid February) until mid-Góa (mid February to mid March).

Galdrastafir 2. Protection

Lífsstafur
(Life Stave)
LBS 4375 8vo 0026v 01

Carve this stave on a piece of Norway spruce and colour it with blood from the right breast, the left hand, and the tongue. It is to be drawn with a merlin (falcon) feather when both the sun and the moon are in the sky.

Lukkuhringur
(Luck Ring)

Carved with human blood on oak, this stave protects against evil spirits.

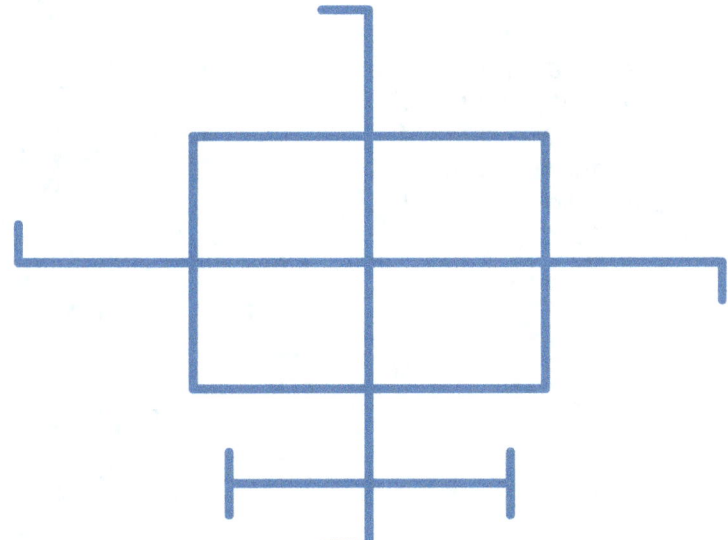

Máni
(Moon)
LBS 4375 8vo 0023v 05

Inscribe on a fox pelt and colour with blood from your right finger and you will not be haunted by ghosts.

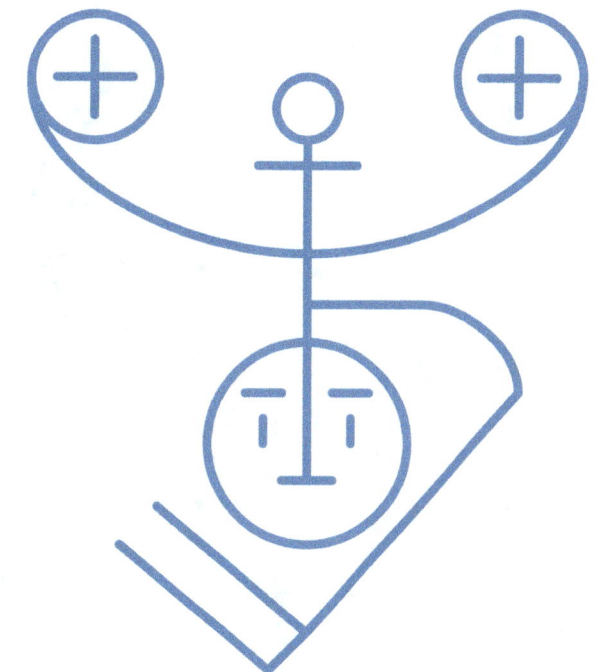

Protection
LBS 2413 8vo 0035r 02

So that you won't get any shame, whatever comes up against you, make this sign with saliva on your forehead with the ring finger of your right hand.

Protection Against Sorcery

Carry this sign with you, it protects from all sorcery.

Return To Sender

Have this sign on calfskin in front of your breast if you want to send back to him that which he has sent to you.

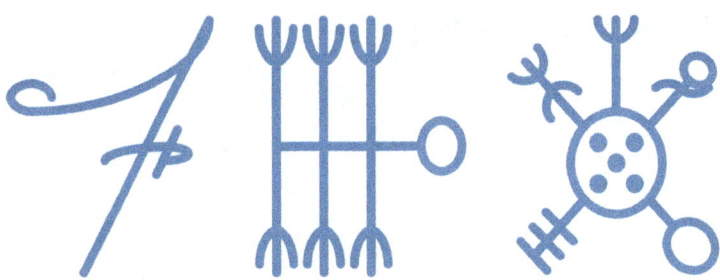

Rosahringur Minni
(Lesser Circle Of Protection)
LBS 4375 8vo 0014r 01

Carve or draw on russet (dark brown with red) fur, *and colour with blood gathered beneath a full moon. It is a good talisman against revenants, sendings, and sorcery.*

Signetshringur
(Signet Ring)

A protective stave.

Galdrastafir   2. Protection

Skjöldur
(Shield)
LBS 4375 8vo 0023v 02

Using a feather from a glaucous gull (Larus Hyperboreus), inscribe this stave on an amnion (the innermost membrane that encloses the embryo of a mammal, bird, or reptile) with blood from your tongue, and you will never perish at sea.

Smjörhnútur
(Butter Knot)

Mark this symbol on butter, and if it is butter made with milk stolen by a Tilberi (a creature created by witches to steal milk), it will coagulate and froth. This may also be carved on silver as an excellent defence against evil harassment whether you keep it with you or use it as a projectile.

Galdrastafir 2. Protection

Sól
(Sun)
LBS 4375 8vo 0023v 06

Inscribe on a pork belly and colour with blood from your nose and tongue, and you will never be cut down by a sword.

Sorcery Prevention
LBS 2413 8vo 0011r 02
LBS 2413 8vo 0031r 02

Draw this stave on parchment with black ink. Keep it near you.

Galdrastafir   2. Protection

Stafir Gegn Galdri
(Staves Against Witchcraft)
LBS 143 8vo 0012v 01

These four symbols guard against all magic from all four directions of the world, and bear them about you.

Stafur Mót Aðsókn Anda 1
(Stave Against Attacks By Spirits 1)
LBS 4375 8vo 0005v 01

Carve this character in oak, and colour them with blood from the little finger of your right hand, and then hang it up over your farmhouse door. The spirits will not enter.

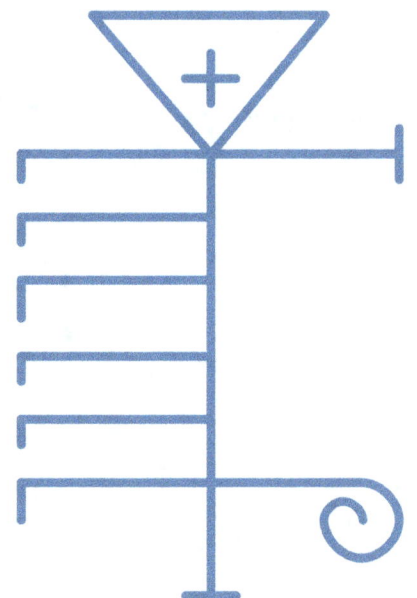

17

Stafur Mót Adsokn Anda 2
(Stave Against Attacks By Spirits 2)
LBS 4375 8vo 0005v 02

Carve this character in oak, and colour them with blood from the little finger of your right hand, and then hang it up over your farmhouse door. The spirits will not enter.

Stafur Mót Adsokn Anda 3
(Stave Against Attacks By Spirits 3)
LBS 4375 8vo 0005v 03

Carve this character in oak, and colour them with blood from the little finger of your right hand, and then hang it up over your farmhouse door. The spirits will not enter.

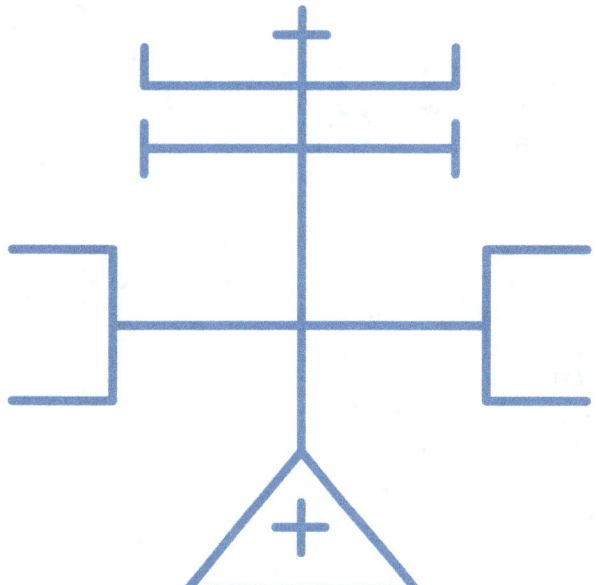

Galdrastafir 2. Protection

Stafur Mót Stefnivargi 1
(Stave Against Stefnvargar and Animal Bites 1)

A stefnivarg is an animal that has been given power by magic and then sent to do harm to someone.

Carve this talisman on oak and place it with an incantation beneath a doorpost, so that your livestock walk over it. Walk three times clockwise and three times anticlockwise around your foreland on the first day of the new moon, fasting, and all alone.

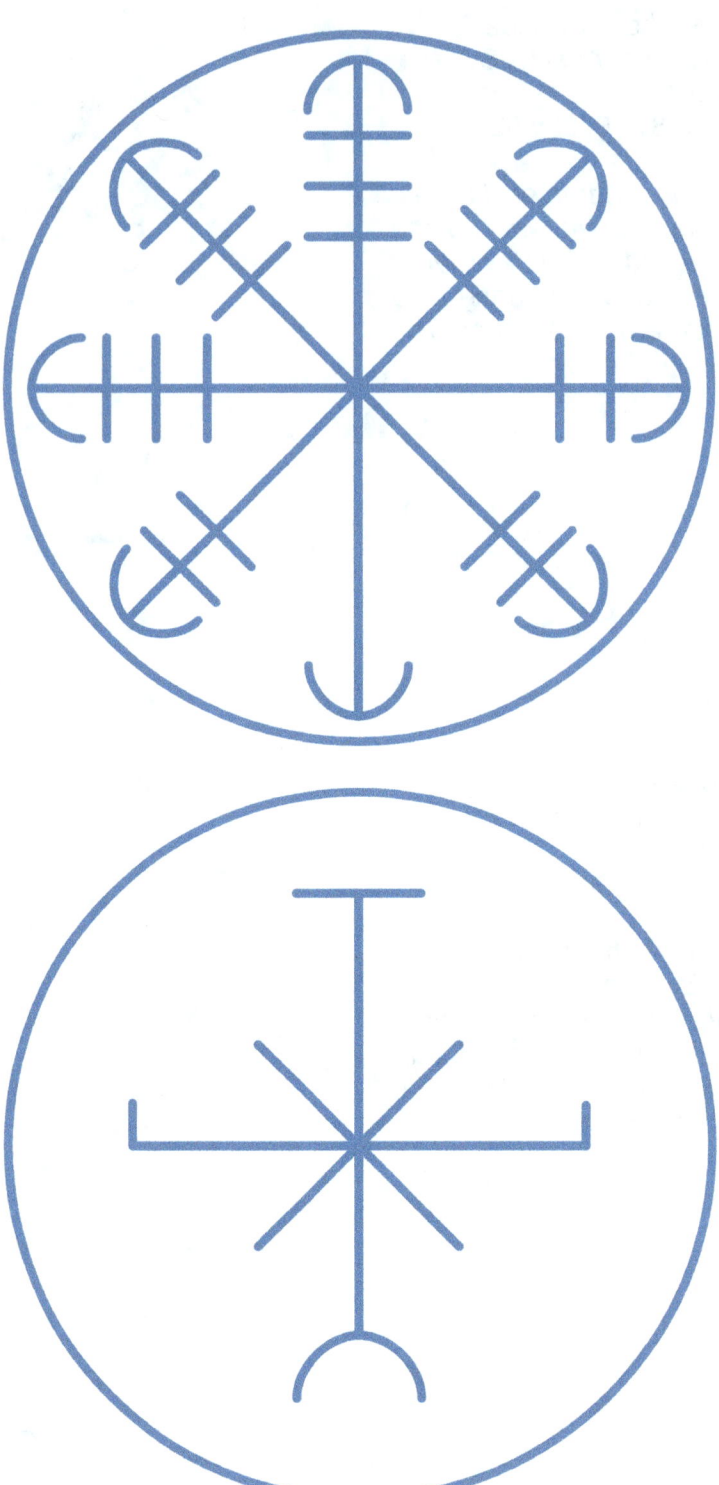

Stafur Mót Stefnivargi 2
(Stave Against Stefnvargar and Animal Bites 2)

A stefnivarg is an animal that has been given power by magic and then sent to do harm to someone.

Carve this talisman on oak and place it with an incantation beneath a doorpost, so that your livestock walk over it. Walk three times clockwise and three times anticlockwise around your foreland on the first day of the new moon, fasting, and all alone.

Stafur Mót Stefnivargi 3
(Stave Against Stefnvargar and Animal Bites 3)

A stefnivarg is an animal that has been given power by magic and then sent to do harm to someone.

Carve this talisman on oak and place it with an incantation beneath a doorpost, so that your livestock walk over it. Walk three times clockwise and three times anticlockwise around your foreland on the first day of the new moon, fasting, and all alone.

Stafur Mót Stefnivargi 4
(Stave Against Stefnvargar and Animal Bites 4)

A stefnivarg is an animal that has been given power by magic and then sent to do harm to someone.

Carve this talisman on oak and place it with an incantation beneath a doorpost, so that your livestock walk over it. Walk three times clockwise and three times anticlockwise around your foreland on the first day of the new moon, fasting, and all alone.

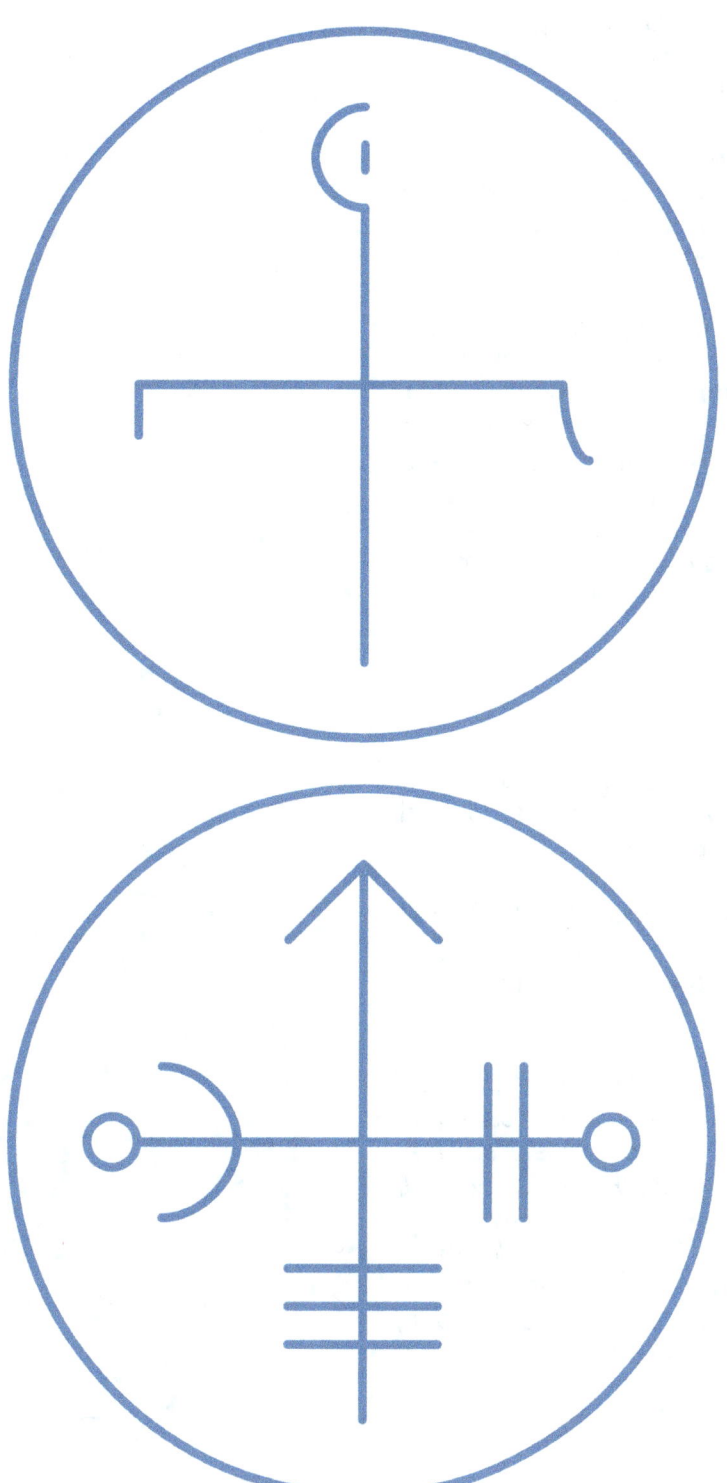

Galdrastafir — *2. Protection*

Stafur Mót Stefnivargi 5
(Stave Against Stefnvargar and Animal Bites 5)

A stefnivarg is an animal that has been given power by magic and then sent to do harm to someone.

Carve this talisman on oak and place it with an incantation beneath a doorpost, so that your livestock walk over it. Walk three times clockwise and three times anticlockwise around your foreland on the first day of the new moon, fasting, and all alone.

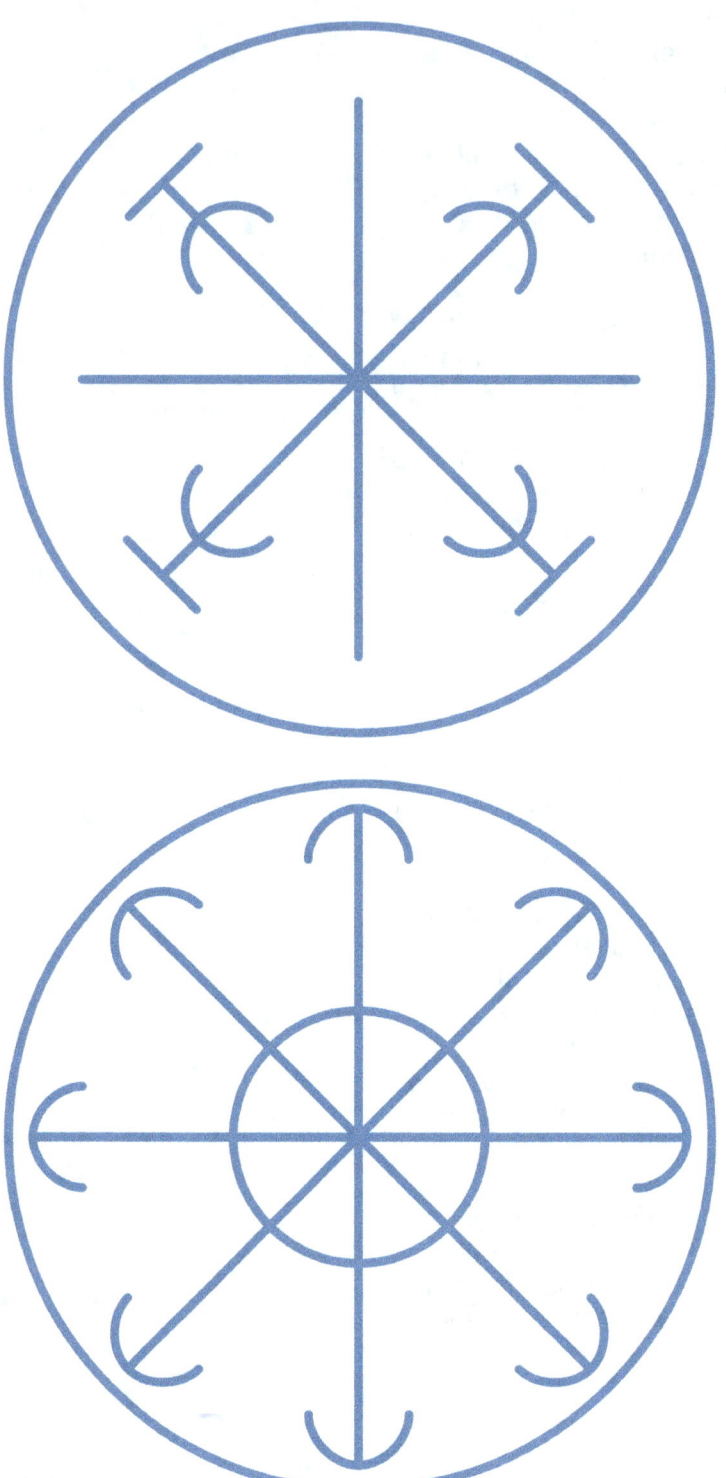

Stafur Mót Stefnivargi 6
(Stave Against Stefnvargar and Animal Bites 6)

A stefnivarg is an animal that has been given power by magic and then sent to do harm to someone.

Carve this talisman on oak and place it with an incantation beneath a doorpost, so that your livestock walk over it. Walk three times clockwise and three times anticlockwise around your foreland on the first day of the new moon, fasting, and all alone.

Galdrastafir   2. Protection

Stafur Mót Stefnivargi 7
(Stave Against Stefnvargar and Animal Bites 7)

A stefnivarg is an animal that has been given power by magic and then sent to do harm to someone.

Carve this talisman on oak and place it with an incantation beneath a doorpost, so that your livestock walk over it. Walk three times clockwise and three times anticlockwise around your foreland on the first day of the new moon, fasting, and all alone.

Stafur Til Að Varna Galdri 1
(Stave To Defend Against Sorcery 1)
LBS 2917a 4to 0017r 01
LBS 4627 8vo 0018v 01
LBS 977 4to 0046v 06

If you wish to be free from all sorcery, inscribe this stave on lead during a waxing moon, and wear it and never remove it.

Stafur Til Að Varna Galdri 2
(Stave To Defend Against Sorcery 2)
LBS 2917a 4to 0025r 02

First walk in three cross-paths and then take three pieces of burning sulphur, which has lain in sacramental wine and vinegar, mixed in equal parts. Sprinkle it on your hands and the soles of your feet. If the ghost is visible, you must confine it within a ring in an out-of-the-way place far from human paths. The entire circle must be lined with burning sulphur. The ghost is then ordered to keep itself inside the ring, until the designated time comes. Take care not to tell anyone of this, because if you do, the action will be ruined.

Sverð
(Sword)
LBS 4375 8vo 0023v 01

Inscribe this stave on lignite (jet stone) and colour it with blood from under the thumb nail of your left hand, and the little toe of your right foot. Wear it in the middle of your chest and you will never be murdered by your enemy.

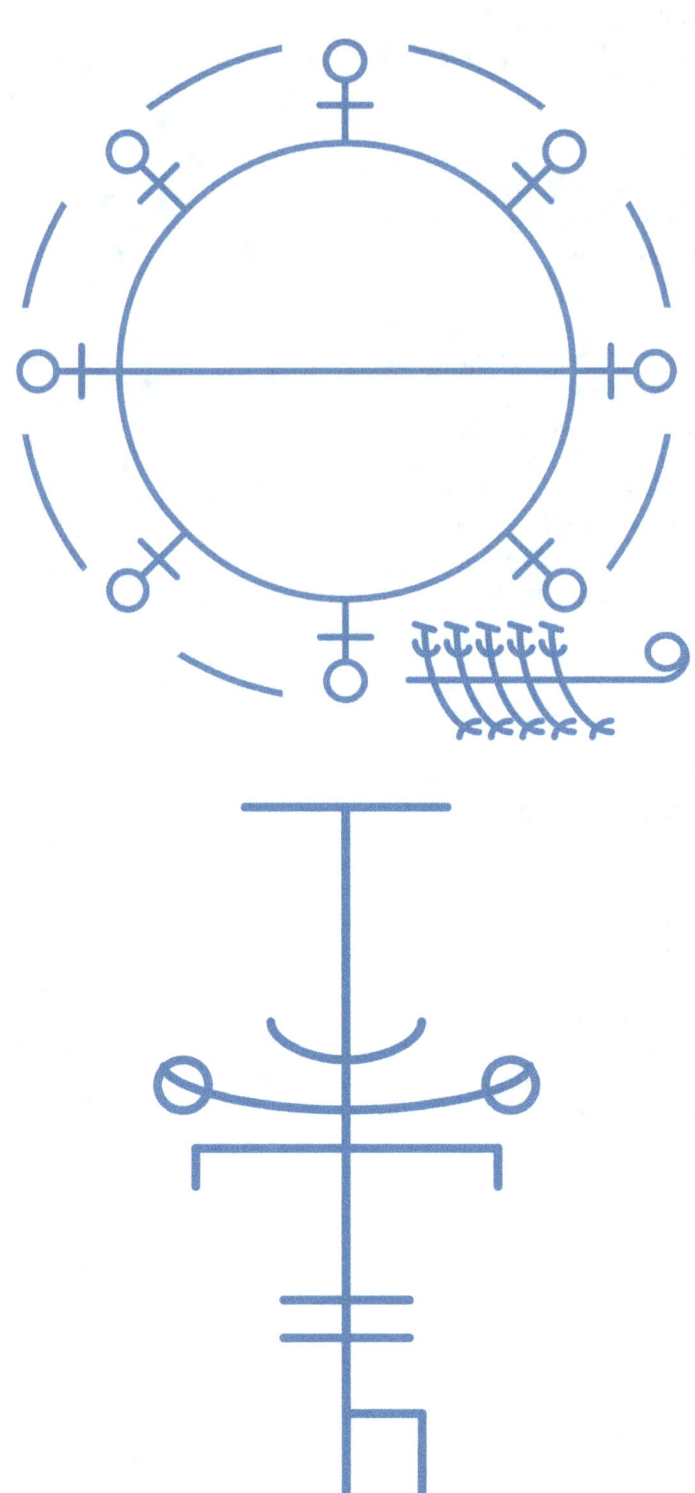

Galdrastafir 2. Protection

Þekkr
(Against Stefnivargar, Both Foxes and Mice)
LBS 4375 8vo 0009v 06

A stefnivarg is an animal that has been given power by magic and then sent to do harm to someone.

Carve this stave with blood on fox pelt, and walk clockwise and anticlockwise over the hills and high verges of your farmland. Recite spells and invocations until all the noxious creatures have been gathered together. Then bind them and kill them.

Þórshamar
(Thor's Hammer)
LBS 2917a 4to 0020v 03
LBS 4375 8vo 0010r 01

This sign is used by magicians to call out thieves and other witcheries.

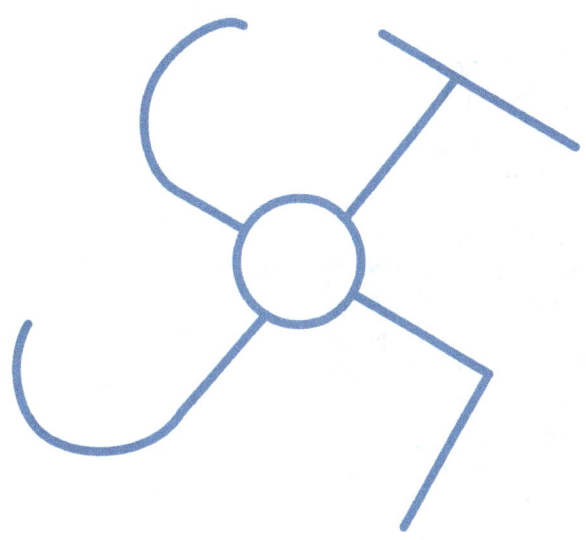

Galdrastafir — 2. Protection

Þrumr
(Against Stefnivargar, Both Foxes and Mice)
LBS 4375 8vo 0009v 03

A stefnivarg is an animal that has been given power by magic and then sent to do harm to someone.

Carve this stave with blood on fox pelt, and walk clockwise and anticlockwise over the hills and high verges of your farmland. Recite spells and invocations until all the noxious creatures have been gathered together. Then bind them and kill them.

Þundr
(Against Stefnivargar, Both Foxes and Mice)
LBS 4375 8vo 0009v 02

A stefnivarg is an animal that has been given power by magic and then sent to do harm to someone.

Carve this stave with blood on fox pelt, and walk clockwise and anticlockwise over the hills and high verges of your farmland. Recite spells and invocations until all the noxious creatures have been gathered together. Then bind them and kill them.

Galdrastafir — 2. Protection

Galdur til að geta hulið sig sjónum
(To Hinder A Person From Coming To Your House)
ATA Amb 2 F 16-26

If you don't want a man to come into your dwelling, then carve this stave into rowan wood when the sun is in her highest stead, and go three times with the sun and three times in a direction contrary to the sun's course around your farm and hold onto the wand of rowan wood onto which the stave has been carved, and onto some sharp thorn grass (thistle) and then lay both of them together up over your door.

Varnarrósin
(Rose Of Protection)

Wear this stave against your bare chest. Draw it on red paper with human blood, and it will guard against spirits and evil sendings.

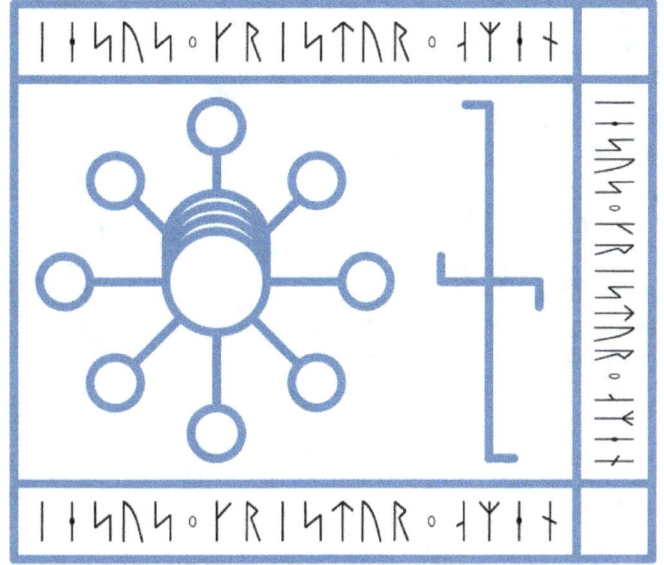

Galdrastafir

2. Protection

Varnarstafur Mót Illum Öndum 1
(Stave Of Protection Against Evil Spirits 1)
LBS 2413 8vo 0030r 01
LBS 2413 8vo 0031v 05
LBS 4375 8vo 0008v 04
LBS 4689 8vo 0010v 01
LBS 977 4to 0033v 06
LBS 977 4to 0040v 13

Inscribe this stave on an amnion (the innermost membrane that encloses the embryo of a mammal, bird, or reptile), using sacramental wine mixed with human blood. Wear them underneath your clothing and you will not be haunted.

Varnarstafur Mót Illum Öndum 2
(Stave Of Protection Against Evil Spirits 2)
LBS 4375 8vo 0008v 05

Inscribe this stave on an amnion (the innermost membrane that encloses the embryo of a mammal, bird, or reptile), using sacramental wine mixed with human blood. Wear them underneath your clothing and you will not be haunted.

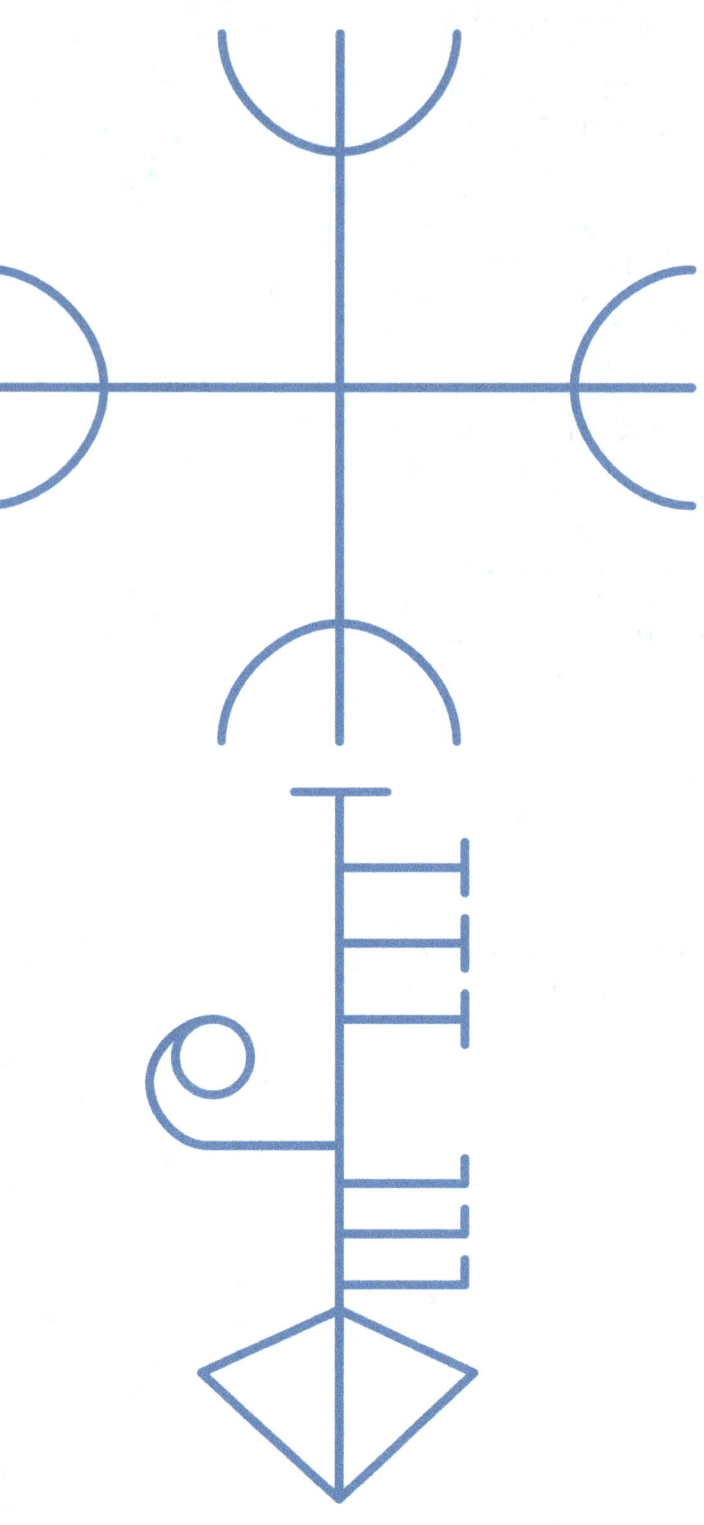

Varnarstafur Mót Illum Öndum 3
(Stave Of Protection Against Evil Spirits 3)

Inscribe this stave on an amnion (the innermost membrane that encloses the embryo of a mammal, bird, or reptile), using sacramental wine mixed with human blood. Wear them underneath your clothing and you will not be haunted.

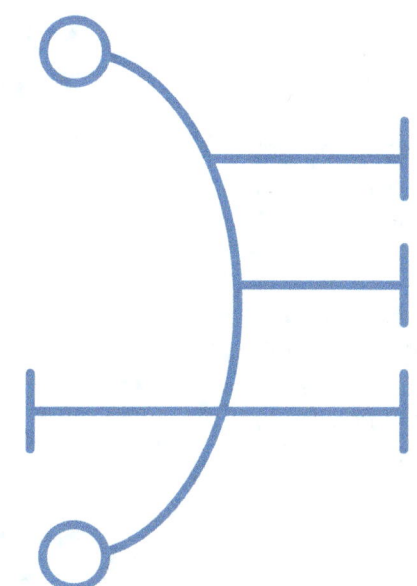

Vatnahlífir
(Protection against drowning)
IB 383 4to 0023r 02
LBS 2917a 4to 0009r 02
LBS 4627 8vo 0018r 01

Wear this sign under your left arm.

Galdrastafir — 2. Protection

Vegvísir
(Waymark)
IB 383 4to 0026v 01
LBS 2917a 4to 0015r 01
LBS 4627 8vo 0017v 01

There are several variations of this stave, the two most common of which are included here.

Carry this stave with you and you will hardly ever lose your way in a storm, or die of exposure, and will find your way even if you are unfamiliar with a place.

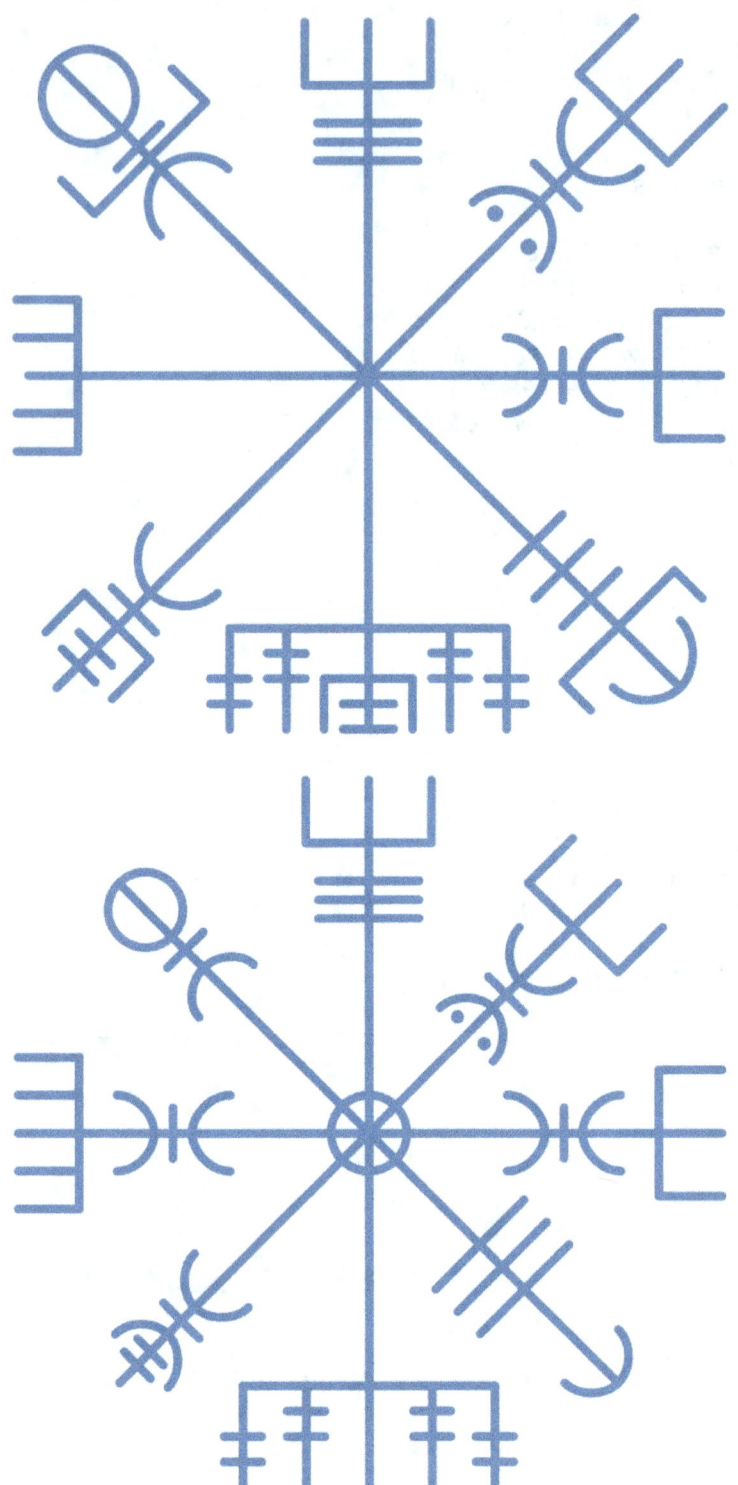

Veldismagn
(Power Amplifier)
LBS 4375 8vo 0022r 02

A power amplifier is to be inscribed on lignite and the grooves coloured with blood, and then placed between your breasts, and you will not suffer evil and will return home safe and sound, whether you travel by sea or land.

Vörn Gegn Hatri
(Protection Against Hatred, Reconciler)
IB 383 4to 0025v 04
LBS 2917a 4to 0014r 02
LBS 4689 8vo 0018v 03
LBS 977 4to 0044v 01

If someone hates you, inscribe these staves on book-velvet, and secretly lay them beneath his head.

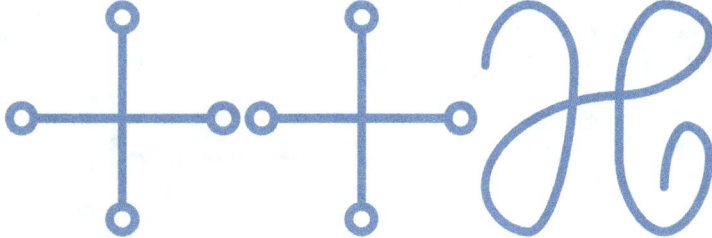

3. Love

**Að Ná Ástum Kvenna
(To Win The Love Of A
Woman)
LBS 2917a 4to 0023r 02**

Carve this stave on oak, and hold it in your hand when you kiss a woman who you long for.

**Að Ná Ástum Kvenna
(To Win The Love Of A
Woman)**

Inscribe this stave on cheese or bread and give it to her to eat without her suspecting.

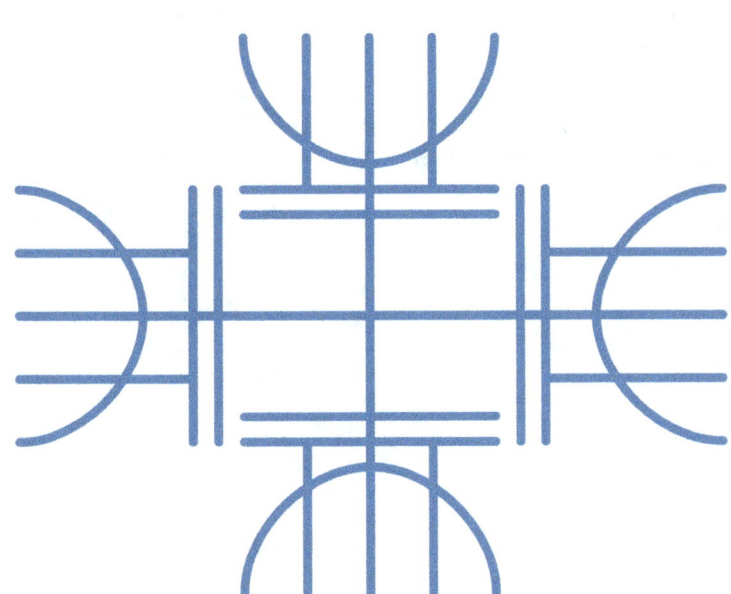

Galdrastafir   3. Love

Að Unni
(To Win a Girl's Heart)
LBS 4375 8vo 0032r 01

Ástarrósin
(Rose of Love)

Inscribe this stave with blood from the palm of your right hand and the girl's mind will be changed if her hand is taken. No one else may be present.

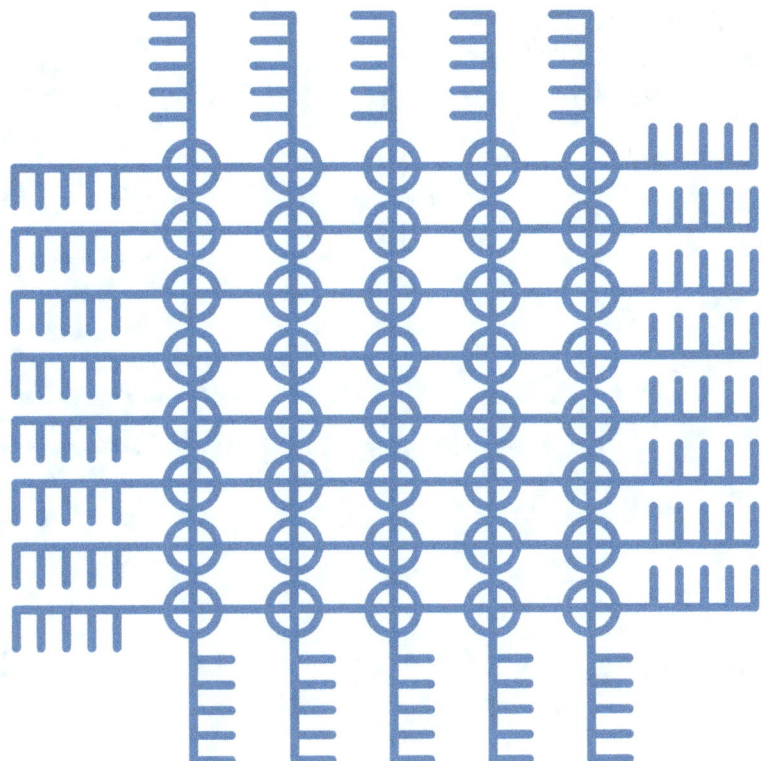

32

Galdrastafir 3. Love

Kvennagaldur
(To Enchant A Woman And Win Her Love)

If you want to bewitch a woman so she will come to no one except you, make a hole in the floor in a place where she will go over it, and pour in some blood and draw a ring of water around it, as well as her name and these staves.

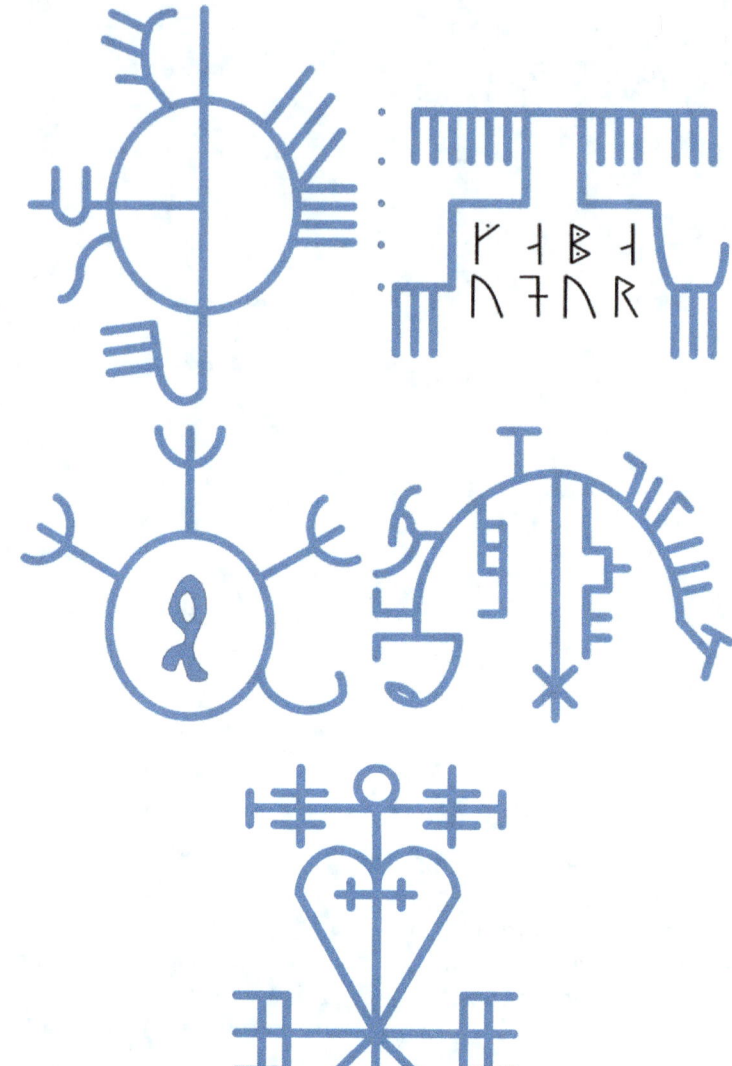

Stafur Til Að Fá Stulku
(Stave To Win A Girl's Heart)
LBS 4375 8vo 0004v 02

33

Galdrastafir 3. Love

Galdur Fái Maður Aðsvif Eða
Faraldur 1
(To Win A Girl's Love 1)
ATA Amb 2 F 16-26
LBS 2413 8vo 0013v 05
LBS 2413 8vo 0031v 03

Galdur Fái Maður Aðsvif Eða
Faraldur 2
(To Win A Girl's Love 2)
ATA Amb 2 F 16-26

While fasting, make this helm of awe with your saliva in your right palm when you visit the girl whom you wish for.

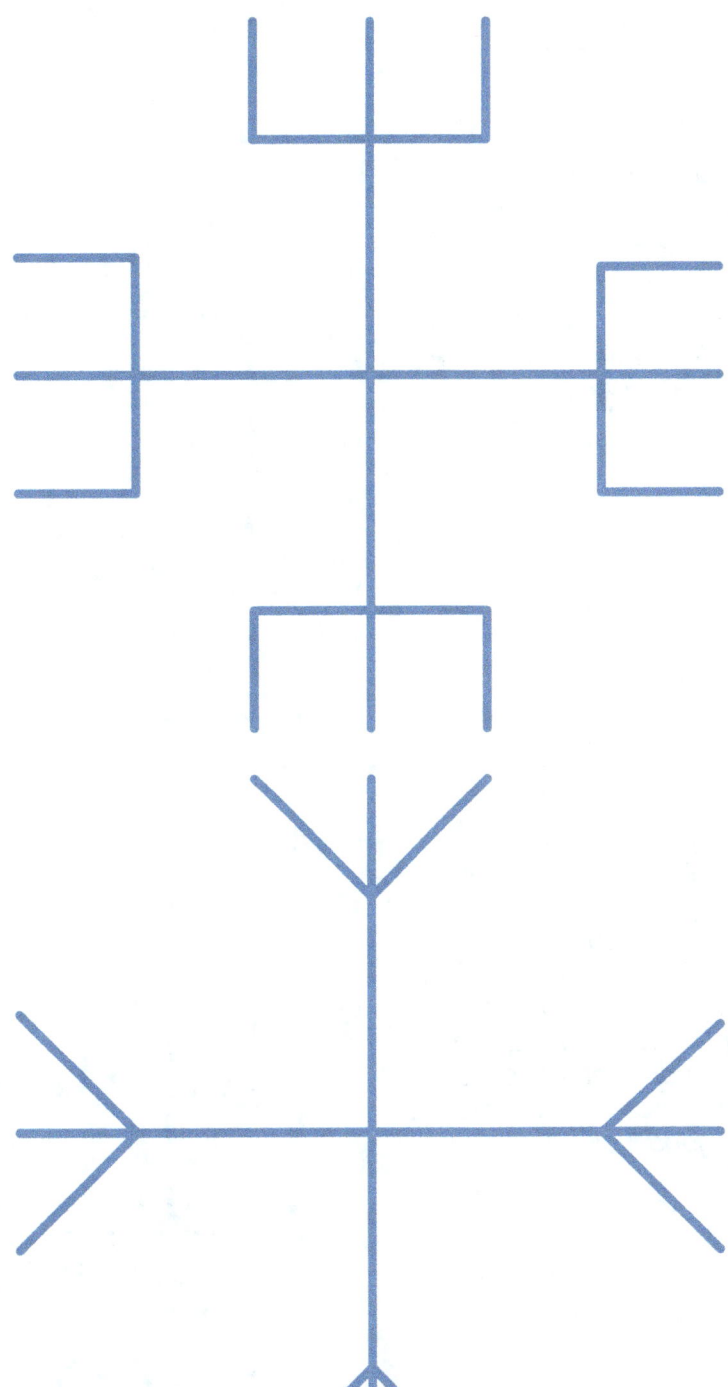

4. Luck

**Lukkustafir
(Luck Staves)
IB 383 4to 0024r 03
LBS 2917a 4to 0010v 02
LBS 4627 8vo 0018r 03**

To prevent all forms of bad luck at sea and on land, carry this stave on your person.

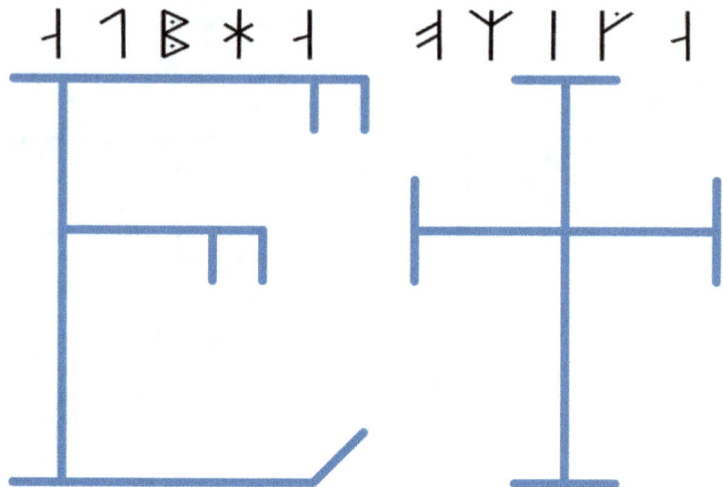

**Heillahnútur (The Good Luck Knot)
LBS 2413 8vo 0037v 01**

This is a man's luck knot. It should be drawn on parchment or carved on metal and carried on your person at all times to ensure good luck.

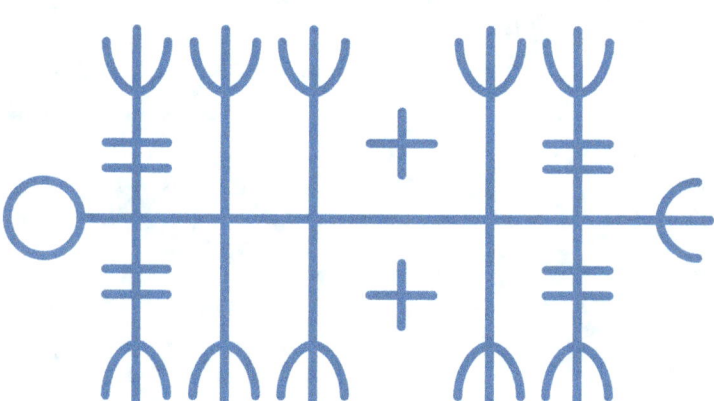

5. Healing

For The Bite Of A Fox

Carve this sign on oak and put it over the house door.

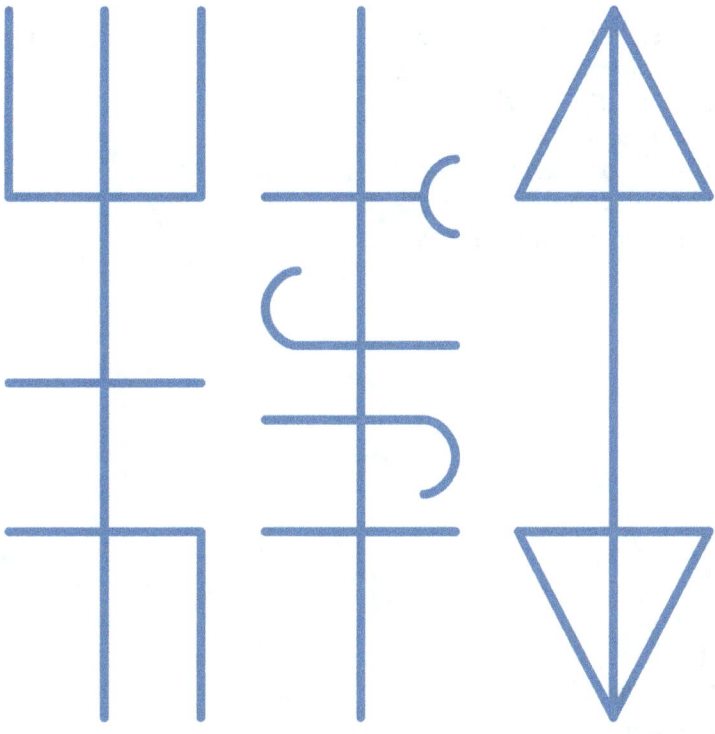

Stafur Við Dýrbiti
(Stave Against Animal Bites)
LBS 4375 8vo 0003r 01

For animal bites, clip this stave on the forehead of one of your wethers (a castrated ram).

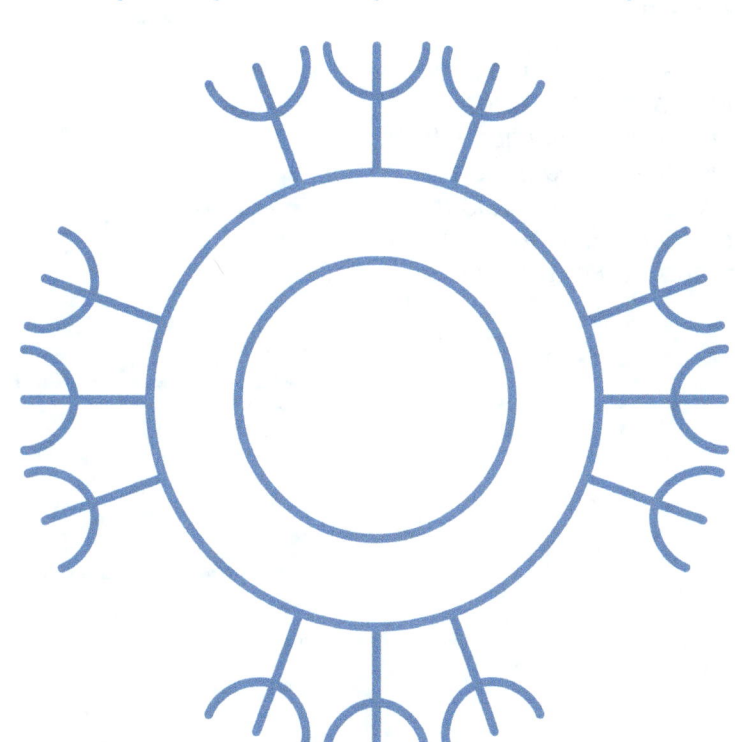

Galdrastafir 5. Healing

Við Dýrbiti
(Against Animal Bites)
LBS 2917a 4to 0031r 02

Herd your sheep into the shed, and then take one wether (a castrated ram), neither the oldest nor the youngest. Carve this stave on oak and colour it with blood, and then tie it to the wether and rattle off a spell over it.

Við Dýrbiti
(Against Animal Bites)
LBS 2917a 4to 0031r 03

Herd your sheep into the shed, and then take one wether (a castrated ram), neither the oldest nor the youngest. Carve this stave on oak and colour it with blood, and then tie it to the wether and rattle off a spell over it.

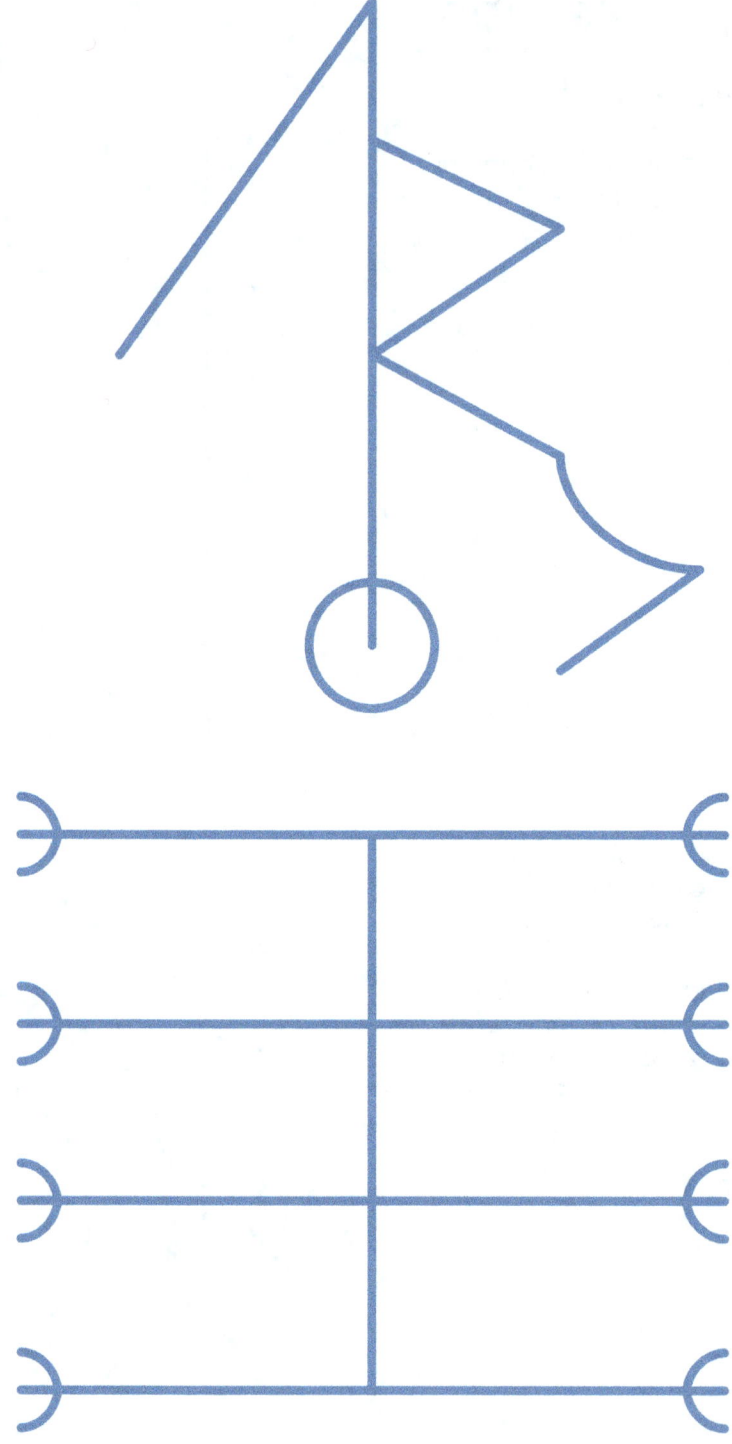

Galdrastafir 5. Healing

Við Dýrbiti
(Against Animal Bites)
LBS 2917a 4to 0031r 04

Herd your sheep into the shed, and then take one wether (a castrated ram), neither the oldest nor the youngest. Carve this stave on oak and colour it with blood, and then tie it to the wether and rattle off a spell over it.

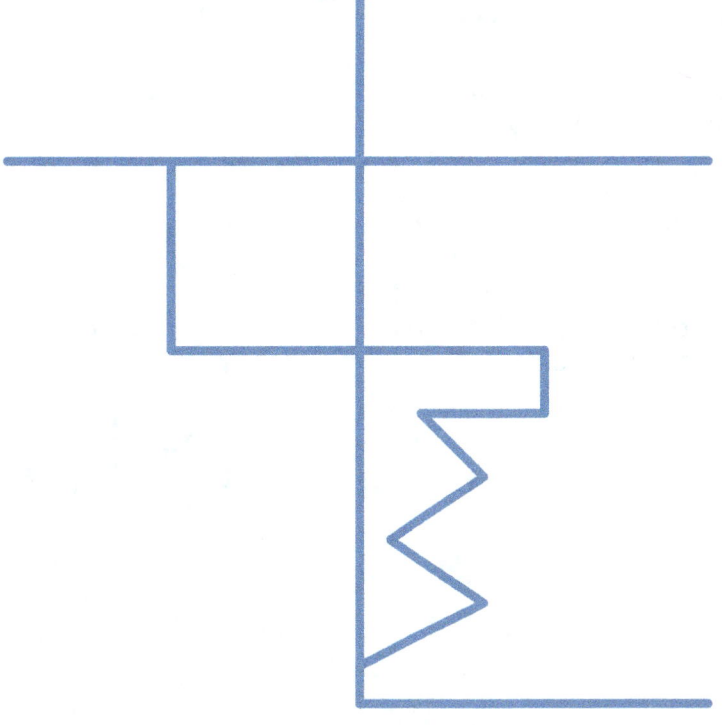

Við Höfuðsundli, Svima
(For Giddiness, Dizziness, And Colic)

Allows no danger to menace you if it is worn. Heals all sorts of ailments.

6. Enhancement

Discovering The Unknown
LBS 2413 8vo 0028r 04

If you desire to know what is concealed from the common folk, carve this stave on brass with a steel instrument and put it near your ear and sleep and you will experience it.

Gapaldur
LBS 2917a 4to 0036r 01

To be worn under the heel of the right foot during bouts of Glíma (Icelandic wrestling).

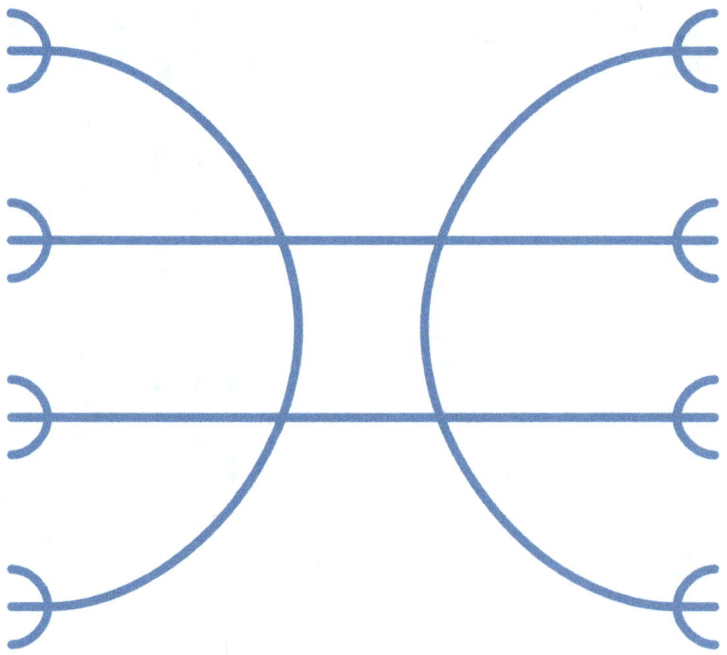

Galdrastafir   6. Enhancement

Ginfaxi
LBS 2917a 4to 0038r 01

To be worn under the toes of the left foot during bouts of Glíma (Icelandic wrestling).

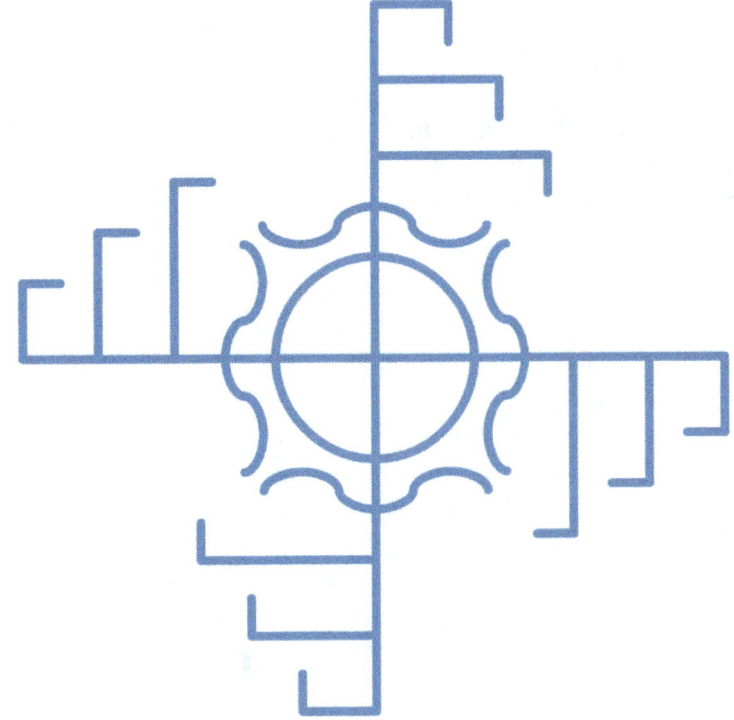

Róðarstafur
(Rowing Stave)
LBS 4375 8vo 0002r 03

Inscribe this stave on leather and colour it with your blood, and then place it beneath the oarlock-pin of the boat's oar. You must personally carry it on and off the boat. No one will then row more powerfully than you.

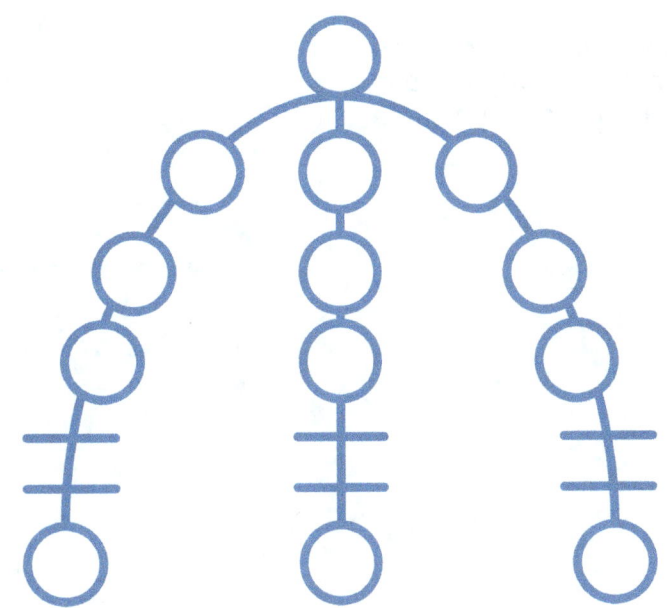

40

Galdrastafir 6. Enhancement

Sláttustafur
(Reaping Stave)
LBS 4375 8vo 0010v 01

This stave is to be carved on the upper nib of a scythe, and coloured with blood from the left hand.

Slátustafur
(Reaping Stave)

This stave is to be carved on the upper nib of a scythe, and coloured with blood from the left hand.

Stafur Til Að Geta Lesið Í
Myrkri
(Stave To Be Able To Read In
The Dark)
LBS 2917a 4to 0021v 02

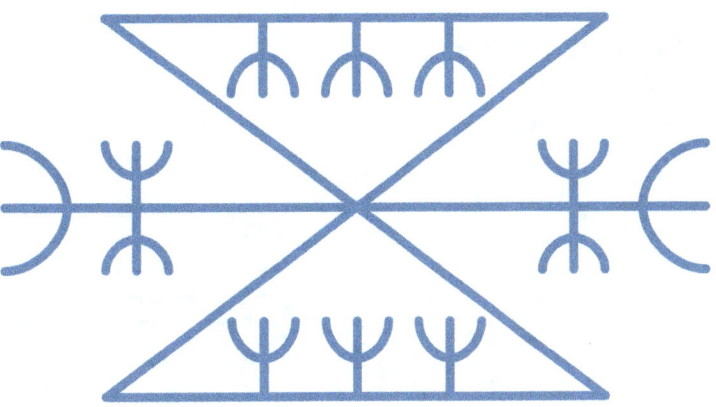

7. Setting Intentions

Að Vinna Hverja Skák
(To Win Every Chess Match)

Carve this stave on oak and keep it in your hand.

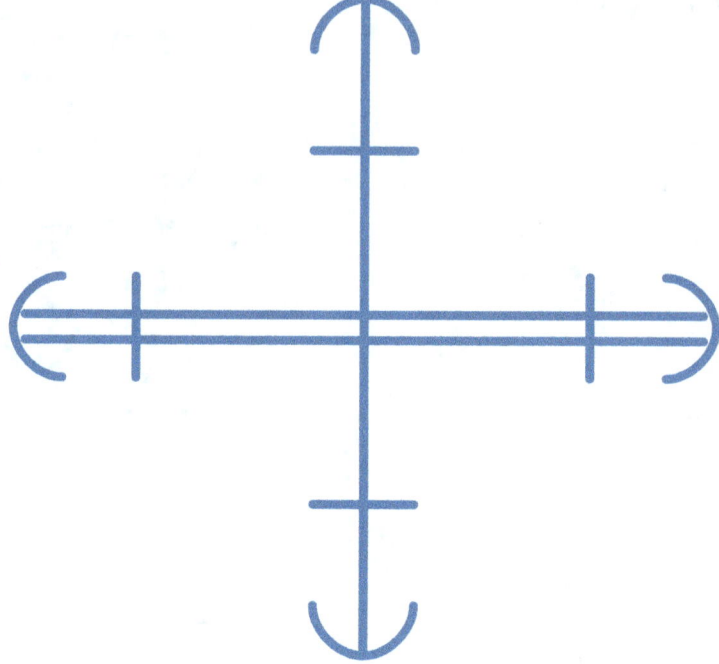

Bænarstafur
(Prayer or Wishing Stave)

If you wish to receive what you ask for, cut this stave into your palm.

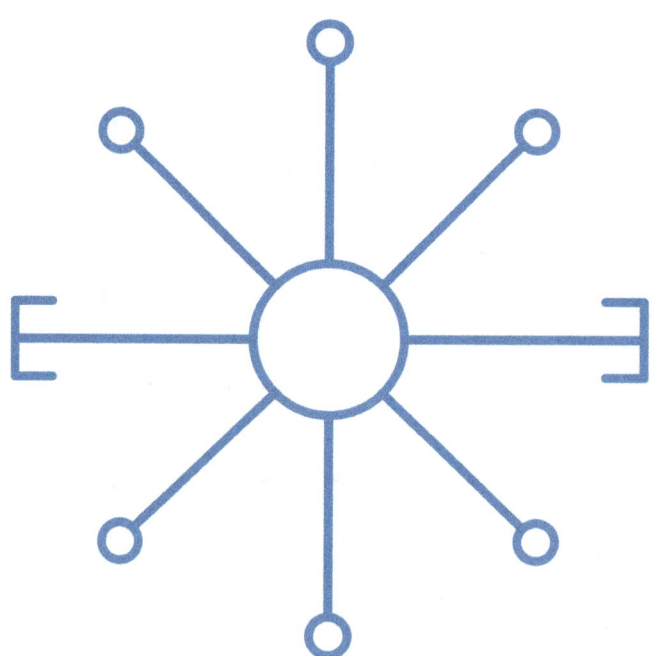

Feingur
(A fertility rune)
IB 383 4to 0024v 03
LBS 2917a 4to 0012r 02
LBS 4627 8vo 0019r 01

If a woman wishes to become pregnant, cut this sign into a piece of cheese and give it to her to eat.

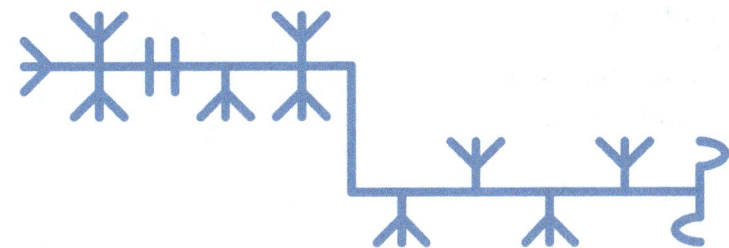

Hjálparhringir Karlamagnúsar
(Charlemagne's Rings of Assistance)
LBS 143 8vo 0008v 01
LBS 143 8vo 0009r 01
LBS 143 8vo 0009v 01
LBS 2917a 4to 0036v 01
LBS 4375 8vo 0006r 01

The first wreath is a defence against every sort of evil swindle, enemy attacks, and despondency.

The second against sudden death and collapse, and all forms of heart-terrors.

The third against the wrath of enemies, to make them tremble in their hearts when they behold the person in possession of the rings, they will become numb and slink away.

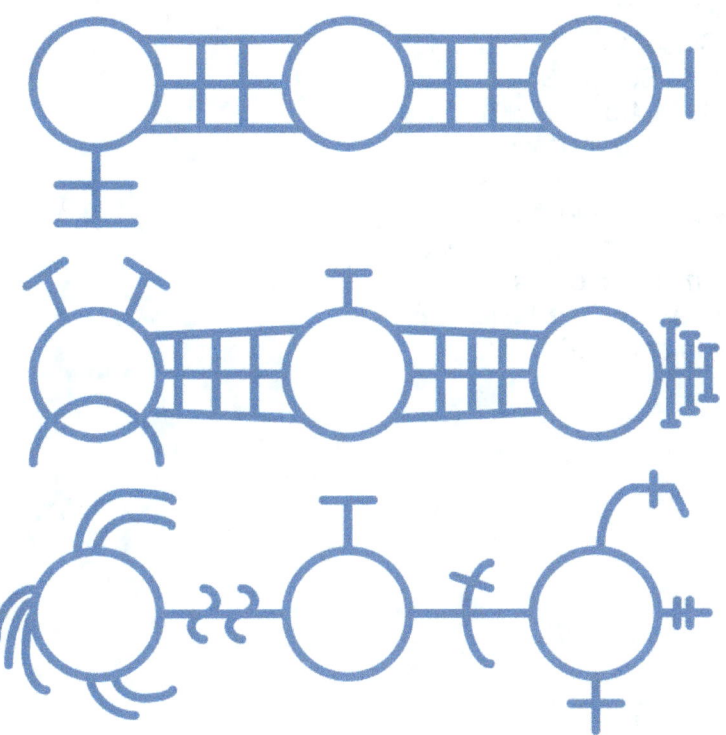

Galdrastafir   7. Setting Intentions

Kaupaloki 1
(Deal Closer 1)
IB 383 4to 0023r 01
LBS 2917a 4to 0009r 01
LBS 4627 8vo 0013v 01

This stave should be cut on a beechwood tablet, and worn between one's breasts, if one wishes to have the better hand in buying and selling.

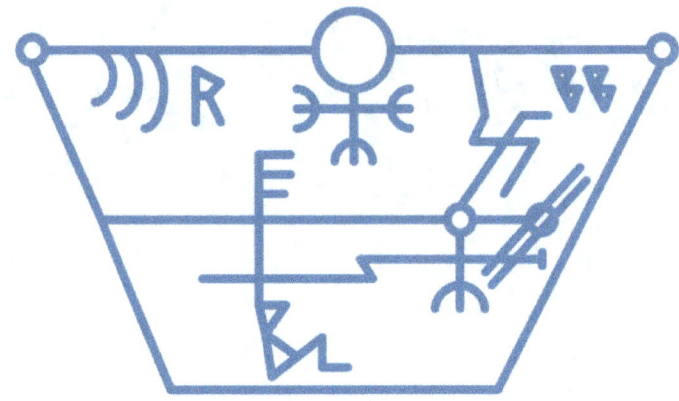

Kaupaloki 2
(Deal Closer 2)
IB 383 4to 0023r 03
LBS 2917a 4to 0009v 01
LBS 4627 8vo 0013v 02

This stave should be cut on a beechwood tablet, and worn between one's breasts, if one wishes to have the better hand in buying and selling.

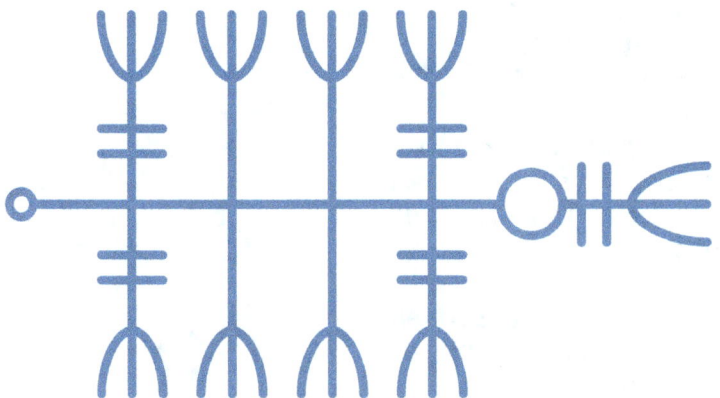

45

Kaupaloki 3
(Deal Closer 3)
LBS 2917a 4to 0020r 01
LBS 4375 8vo 0009v 07
LBS 4627 8vo 0010r 02

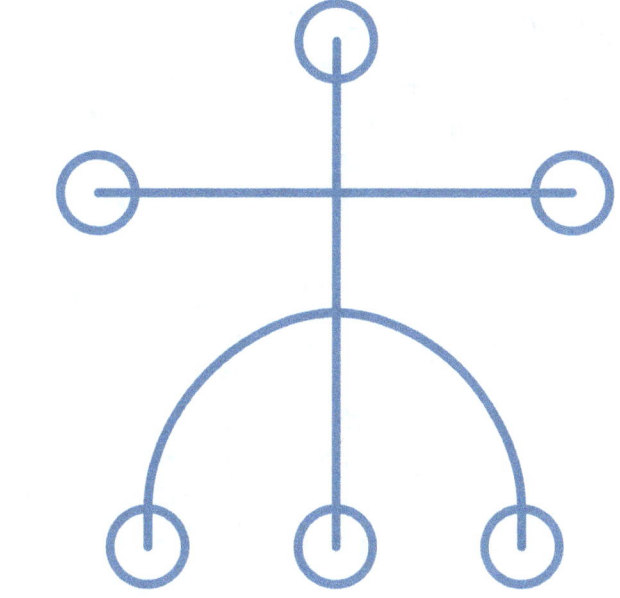

Sigurmerki
(Victory Sign)
LBS 2917a 4to 0017v 01

Use on promontories (headlands) against fog and adverse weather.

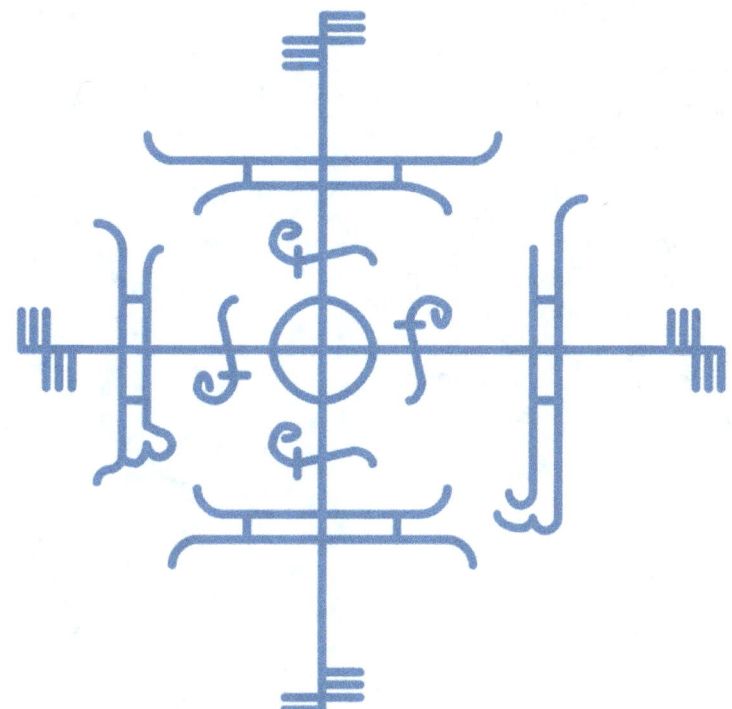

Success
LBS 2917a 4to 0021r 03

Have this sign on grey paper under your left arm when you are talking to somebody and you will have success with them.

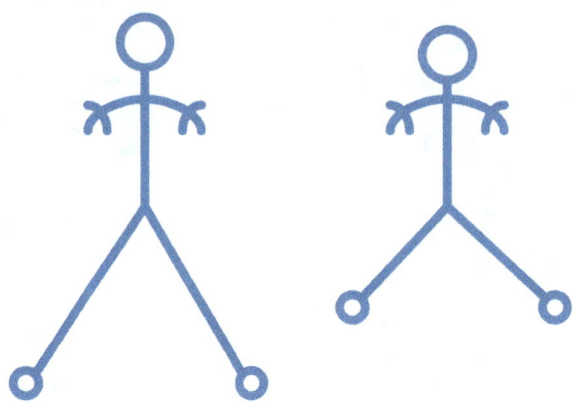

To Acquire The Object You Crave
LBS 2413 8vo 0010v 01
LBS 4689 8vo 0017r 02
LBS 977 4to 0038v 01

Carve this stave in lead and have it in your hand, whichever one you want. Carve it with your food knife and read this verse: 'Da nobis Hodied dim: timi ej Petoribus Haftrus men Inducas'.

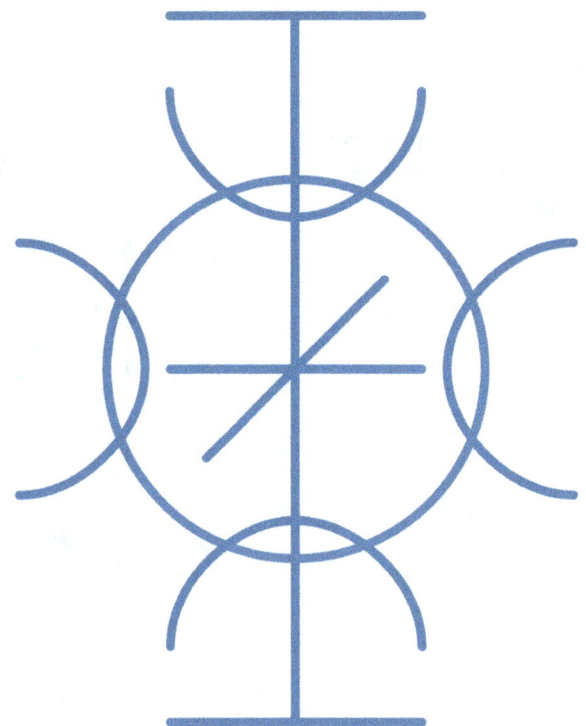

To Get Your Own Wish
LBS 2413 8vo 0008v 02

To Have Success In Business
LBS 2413 8vo 0009v 02

Write this stave on parchment or carve it into oak wood. Keep this stave in your hand when doing business. You will have success.

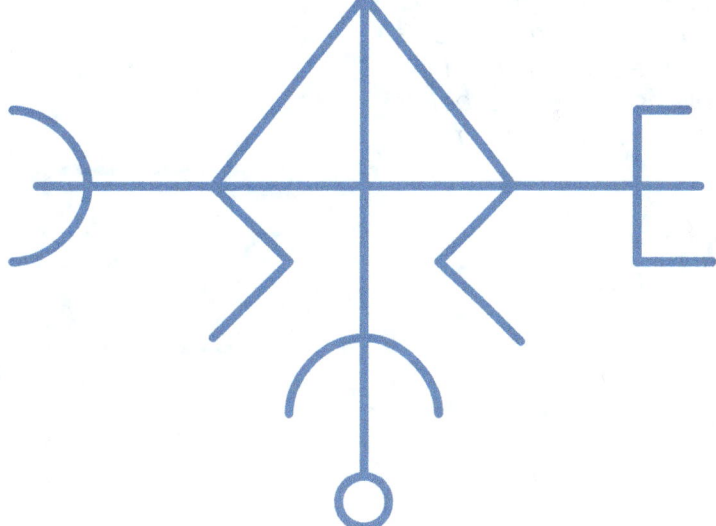

To Overcome Enemies

When you carry these staves with you, you will surely overcome your enemies.

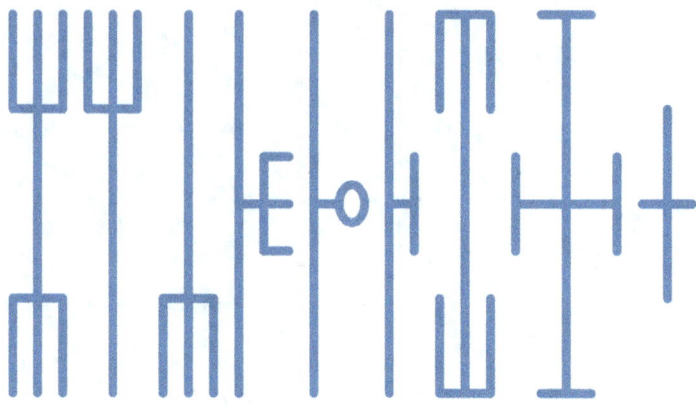

To Win A Debate
LBS 2413 8vo 0020r 01

Write this stave with your saliva while you are fasting ans put it under your left arm if you don't want anyone to get the better of you in a debate or argument.

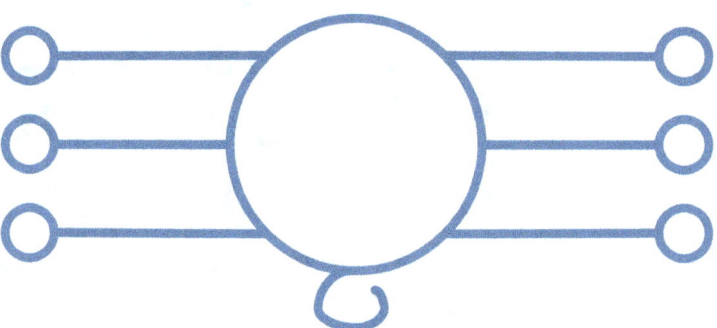

Umbótarstafur
(Stave Of Ameliorations)
LBS 2917a 4to 0022v 01

To relieve the effect of spells and make amends, and for peace and consolation. It is also an excellent protective stave.

Victory In Business With All People

Draw this sign on blotting paper and wear it under your left arm and let no one know that you have it.

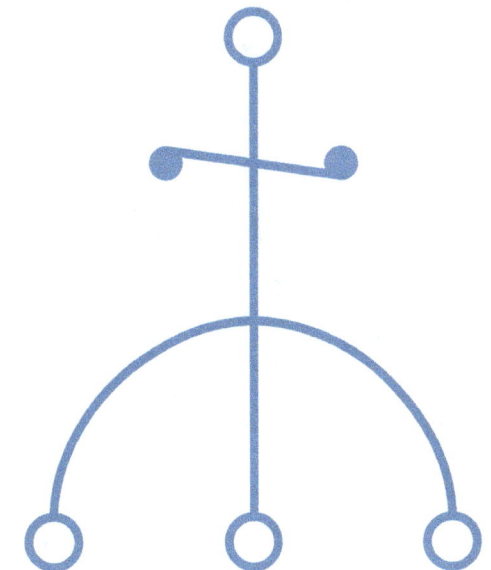

Galdrastafir — 7. Setting Intentions

Victory

Draw this helm of awe on a disc of lead and press it to your forehead between your eyebrows and say 'I bear the helm of awe between my brows!'. You will have victory in every struggle, the powerful will love you, and your enemies will be struck with terror. Victory is assured.

8. Sleep & Dreams

Against Sleeplessness And Bad Dreams

Carve this sign with magnetised iron on a piece of coal.

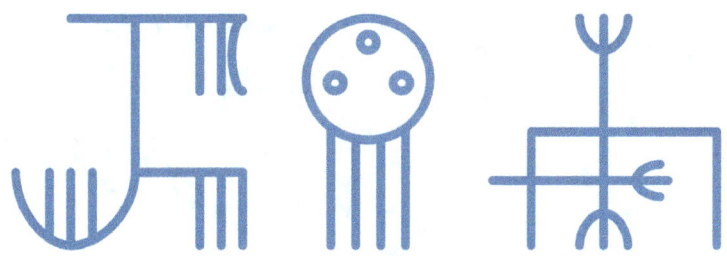

Draumstafir Hinir Mestu
(Greatest Dream Staves)
IB 383 4to 0024r 01
LBS 2917a 4to 0011r 01
LBS 4627 8vo accMat08v 03

If one inscribes these characters on silver or a white hide on Midsummer's Night, and sleeps on them, one will dream what one wishes, when the sun is at its lowest point.

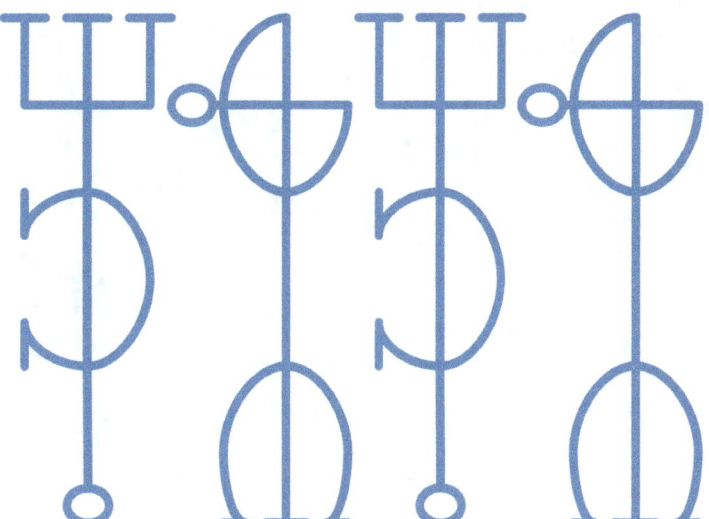

Galdrastafir   8. Sleep and Dreams

Draumstafur
(Dream Stave)
LBS 4375 8vo 0001r 01

This stave is to be carved on lignite (jet stone) with the spine of a dogfish when the moon is three nights old, and placed beneath your head. You will then dream whatever you wish.

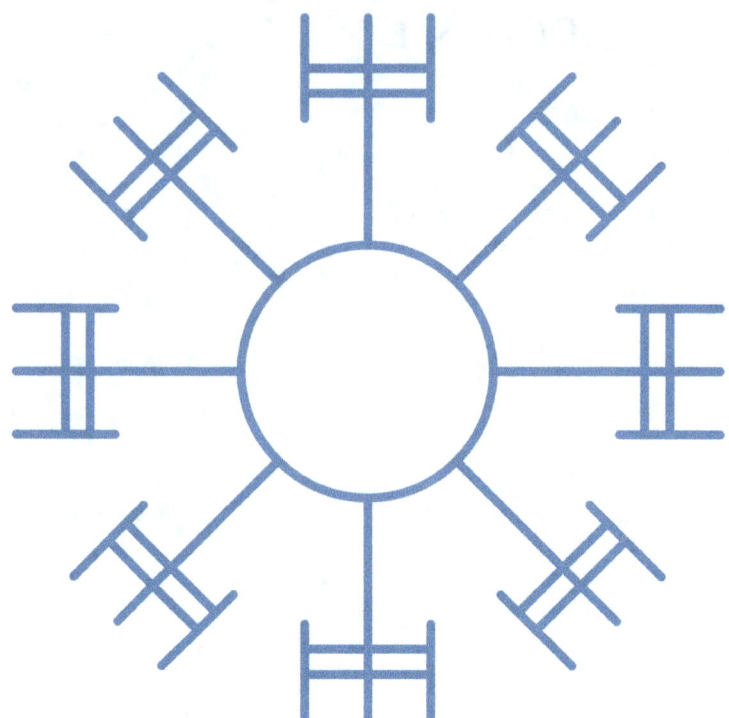

Draumstafur Hinn Meiri
(Greater Dream Stave)
IB 383 4to 0023v 02
LBS 2917a 4to 0010r 01
LBS 4627 8vo accMat08v 02

Carve this stave on Norway spruce, and sleep on it.

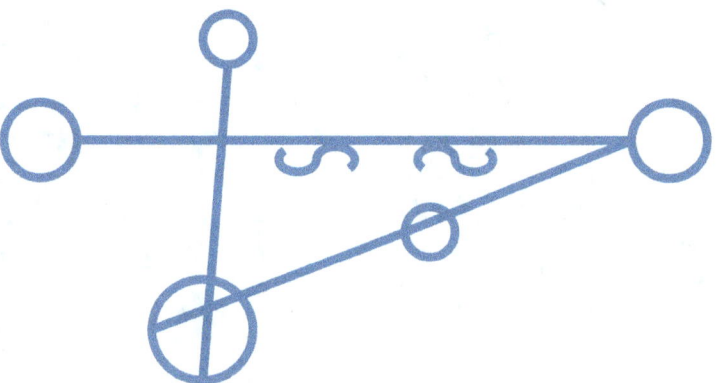

Draumstafur Hinn Minna
(Lesser Dream Stave)
IB 383 4to 0023v 03
LBS 2917a 4to 0010r 02

This stave is to be carved on oak and laid beneath the head of the one who wishes to dream.

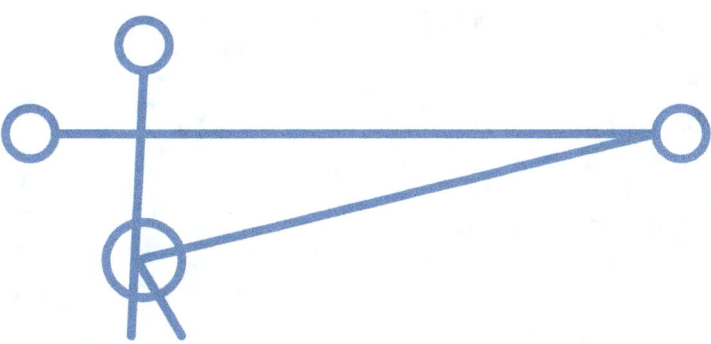

Svefnþorn
(Sleep-Thorn)
IB 383 4to 0024r 02
LBS 2917a 4to 0010v 01

There are several variations of this stave, the two most common of which are included here.

Carve on oak and colour the grooves with your own blood, and then place it in secret on the crown of a man's head.

Svefnþorn 2
(Sleep-Thorn 2)
LBS 4375 8vo 0001v 04

Carve on oak and colour the grooves with your own blood, and then place it in secret on the crown of a man's head.

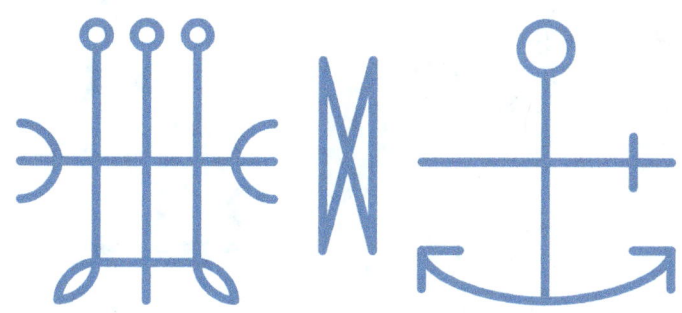

Galdur Til Að Svæfa Mann
(To Make Someone Go To Sleep)

If you want to put someone to sleep, then carve these staves in alder wood and lay it under his head and he will surely sleep until you take it away.

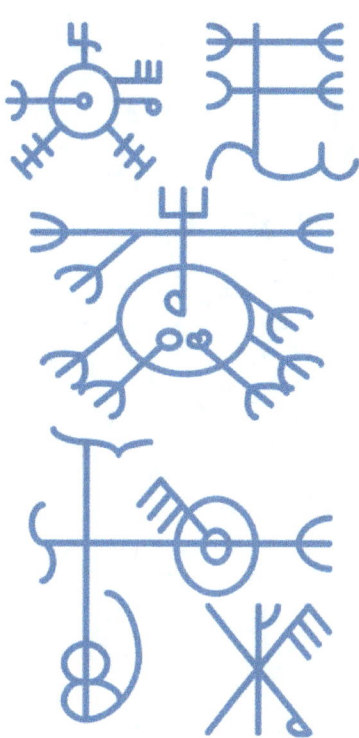

9. Fishing

**Fiskistafur 1
(Fish Stave 1)**

Inscribe this stave on your sinker (lead weight), and you will always have good catches, even when others' are small.

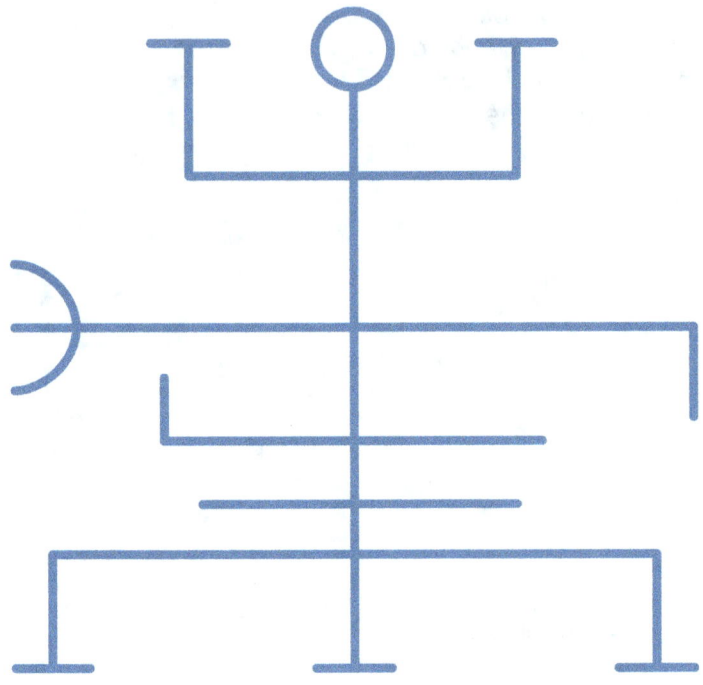

**Fiskistafur 2
(Fish Stave 2)**

Inscribe this stave on your sinker (lead weight), and you will always have good catches, even when others' are small.

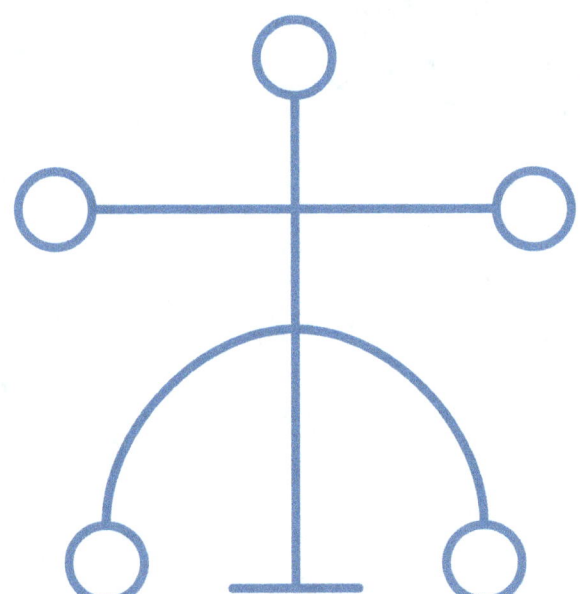

Galdrastafir 9. Fishing

Stafur Til Að Fiska Vel 1
(Stave For Fishing Well 1)
LBS 4375 8vo 0025r 01

Inscribe this stave on calfskin or on the hook-sinker itself.

Stafur Til Að Fiska Vel 2
(Stave For Fishing Well 2)
LBS 4375 8vo 0025r 02

Inscribe this stave on calfskin or on the hook-sinker itself.

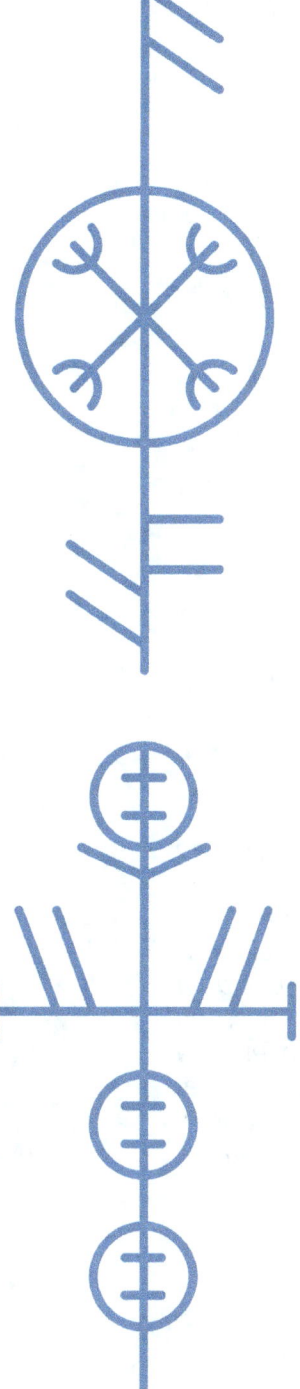

Galdrastafir 9. Fishing

Stafur Til Að Fiska Vel 3
(Stave For Fishing Well 3)
LBS 4375 8vo 0025r 03

Inscribe this stave on calfskin or on the hook-sinker itself.

Veiðistafur
(Fishing Stave)
LBS 4375 8vo 0004v 03

This stave is to be drawn on an amnion (the innermost membrane that encloses the embryo of a mammal, bird, or reptile), *with blood, using a raven's feather pen. It is then to be placed in the gimlet hole beneath the bow of a boat that is going to sea to fish, and it will always have a good catch.*

59

10. Staves Against Theft

Stafur Til Að Sjá Þjóf 1
(Stave For Seeing A Thief 1)
LBS 2917a 4to 0035r 03
LBS 4375 8vo 0008v 03
LBS 4627 8vo 0014r 02
LBS 4689 8vo 0019r 04
LBS 977 4to 0032v 03
LBS 977 4to 0037v 05

This stave is to be inscribed on the bottom of a washbasin with a chip from a basalt slab. Burn juniper to ash and use it to colour the stave, then put it in the water, and you will see the thief.

Stafur Til Að Sjá Þjóf 2
(Stave For Seeing A Thief 2)
LBS 2917a 4to 0033v 02
LBS 2917a 4to 0035r 02
LBS 4375 8vo 0008v 01

This stave is to be inscribed on the bottom of a washbasin with a chip from a basalt slab. Burn juniper to ash and use it to colour the stave, then put it in the water, and you will see the thief.

Stafur Til Að Sjá Þjóf 3
(Stave For Seeing A Thief 3)
LBS 4375 8vo 0002v 02

Inscribe this stave three times with blood, and then sleep on the stave an entire night. You will see the thief in your sleep.

Þjófastafur 1
(Thief Stave 1)
AM 434 a 12mo 0004v 01

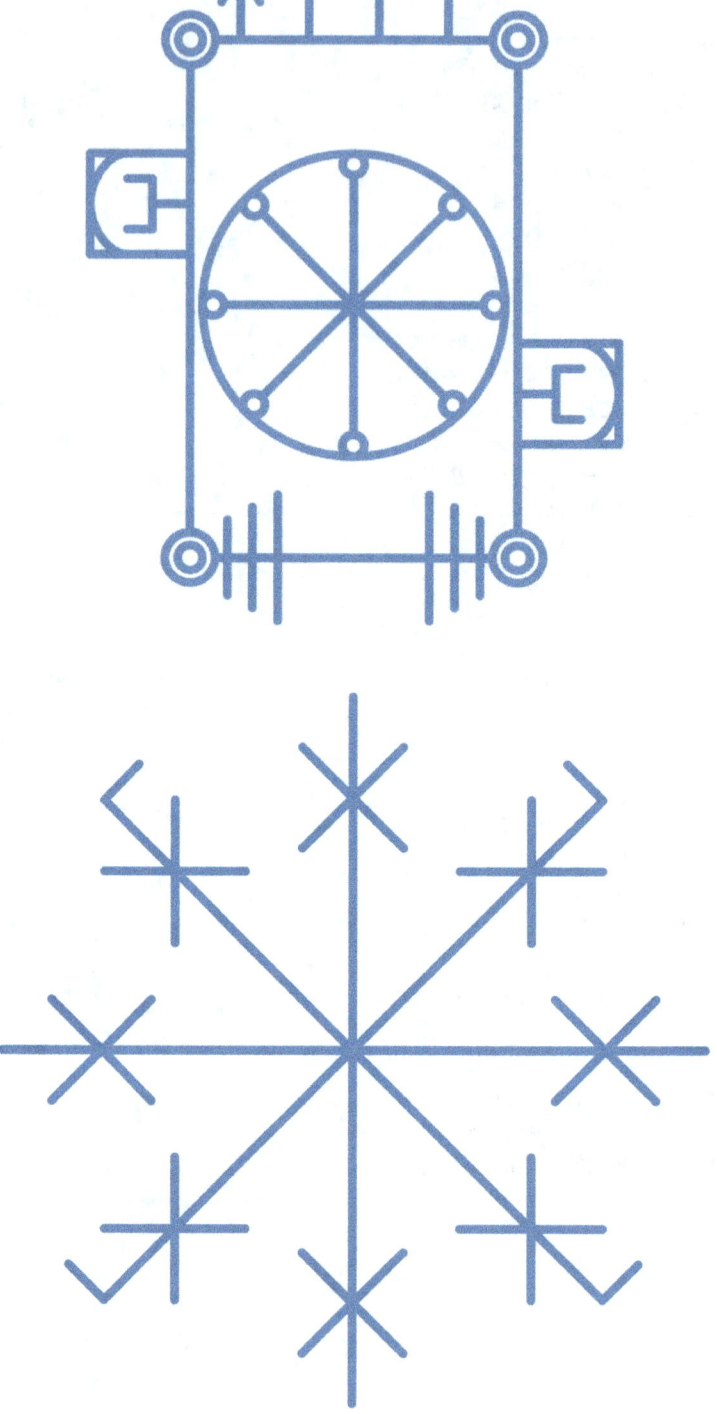

Þjófastafur 2
(Thief Stave 2)
IB 383 4to 0025r 01
LBS 2917a 4to 0012v 01

Put this sign under the threshold of your enemy and he will collapse when he steps over it if he has committed an act of thievery against you.

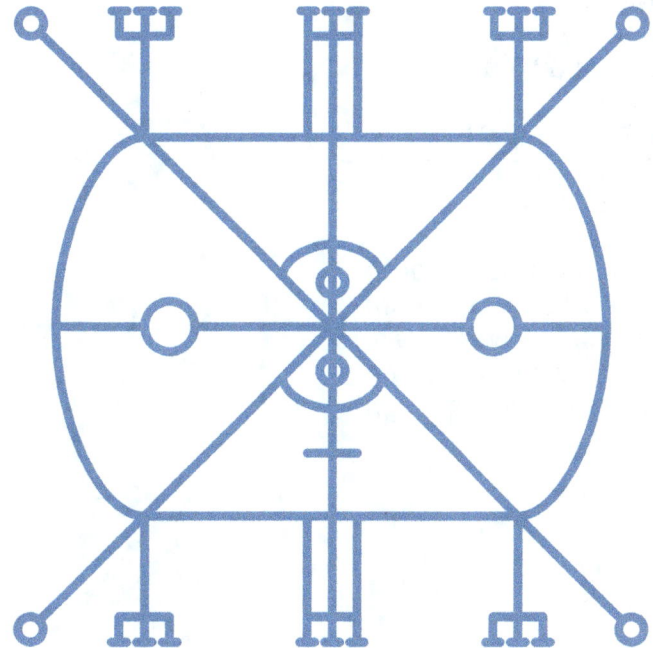

Þjófastafur 3
(Thief Stave 3)
IB 383 4to 0025r 02
LBS 2917a 4to 0013r 02
LBS 4627 8vo 9999r-RB 01

If you want someone to steal, then carve this sign on the bottom of the (wooden) plate he eats off.

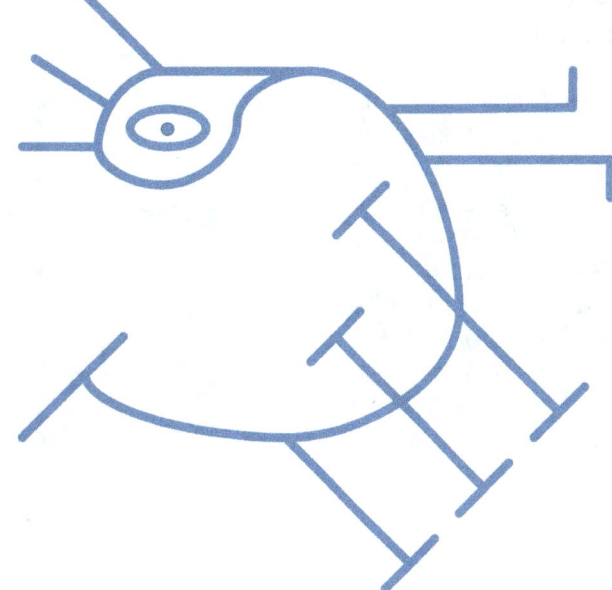

Þjófastafur 4
(Thief Stave 4)
IB 383 4to 0026v 02
LBS 2413 8vo 0004r 01
LBS 2917a 4to 0015v 01
LBS 4627 8vo 0014v 01
LBS 4627 8vo accMat08v 01
LBS 4689 8vo 0017r 01

To discover who is stealing from you, inscribe this stave on the bottom of a washbasin, outside and in, with lead, when the moon is full and at high tide.

Þjófsá
(Thief Revealer)
LBS 2917a 4to 0011v 02
LBS 4627 8vo 0022r 01

If you wish to know who has stolen from you, take the millefolium (yarrow) on Midsummer's Eve and place it in water over which no bird has flown that day, then put it in an unused container and inscribe this stave on the bottom of it. If the plant floats, it is a woman. If it sinks, it is a man. The shadow reveals the person.

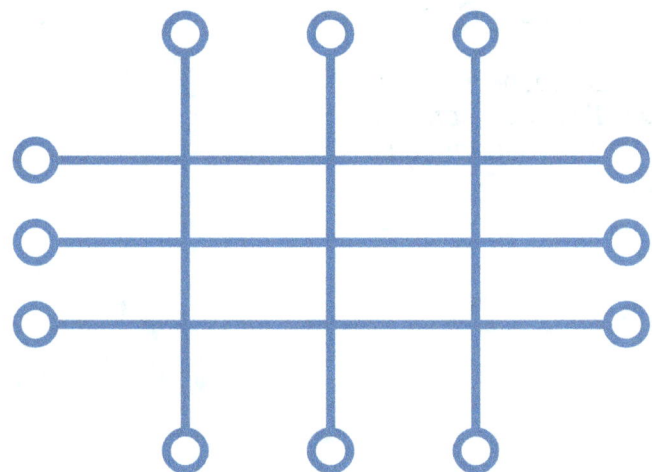

Galdrastafir   *10. Staves Against Theft*

Þjófagaldur 1
(To Discover A Thief 1)

In case of theft you should carve these staves on the bottom of a dish of ashwood, put water in it and strew millefolium (yarrow) into the water and say: 'This I ask according to the nature of the herb and great might of the staves, that the shade of the one who has taken it appear in the water, and that the name of this person be carved on fish gill with etin's bewilderments (mirk runes to be carried on yourself), and carry these on yourself and say: Oðin, Loki, Frò, Baldur, Njorðr, Tyr, Birgur, Hoenir, Freyja, Gefjun, Gusta, and all those gods and goddesses who dwell and have dwelt in Valholl from the beinings of heaven, and they must help me so that I will have success in this matter'.

Þjófagaldur 2
(To Discover A Thief 2)

Draw blood from above the nail of your left middle finger and draw this sign on paper. Have a cat hair on the back side of it. Stick it under your cap and sleep with it by the old moon until you dream of him.

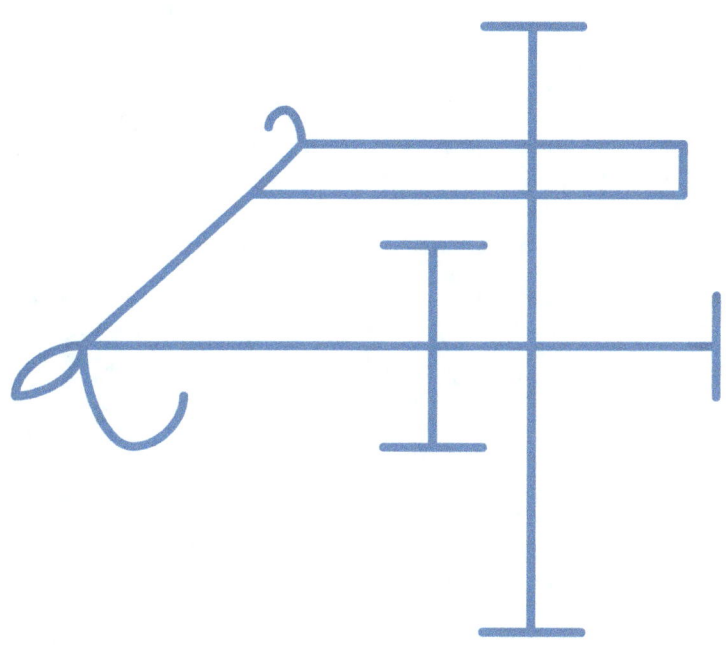

To Find Out A Thief
ATA Amb 2 F 16-26

Carve this on oak and lay it under the turf on top of a grave and let it lie there.

Galdur Sem Veldur Spýju
(To Find Out A Thief)
ATA Amb 2 F 16-26

Carve these on a man's leg bone and then he will come and spit out whosoever stole from you.

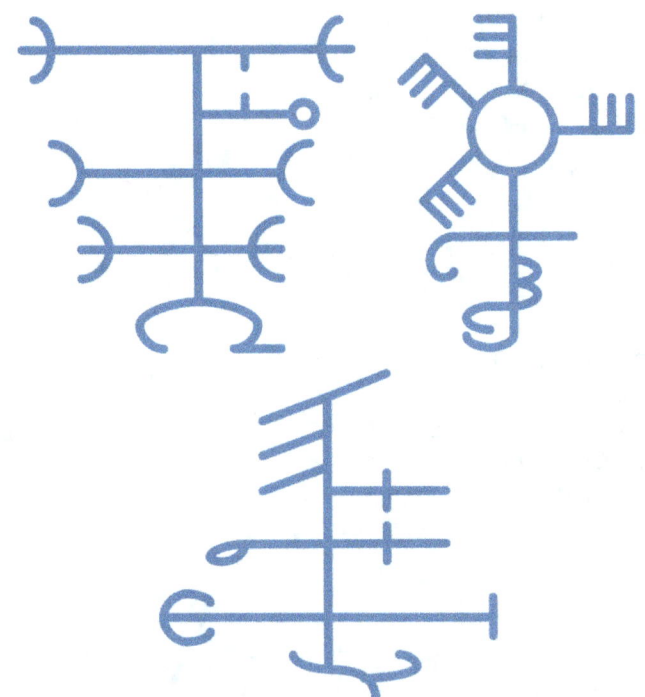

Galdrastafir   *10. Staves Against Theft*

Galdur Til Að Afhjúpa Þjóf
(To Find Out A Thief)
ATA Amb 2 F 16-26

Make this stave with chalk on the cross-beam of the house from which the thing was stolen; then stick a copper pin in the right eye [of the stave] and say IN BUSKAN LUCANUS and FORTUM ATUM EST.

To Uncover A Thief

If anyone would like another way to find out who is stealing from him, then he should make this stave on the bottom of a bowl with a wooden handled knife. Raise blood from under your big toe and your right hand and spread it around the stave. Then take fresh water and put millefolium (yarrow) into it. The water should be drawn after midnight on St John's Night (23rd June) and taken with gloves so that it gets on your hands. The plant should be anointed with blood, as should these three staves.

11. Legal

Dunfaxi
(Down-Mane, To Win a Law Case)

If you want to win a law case, carry this sign with you on a piece of new oak.

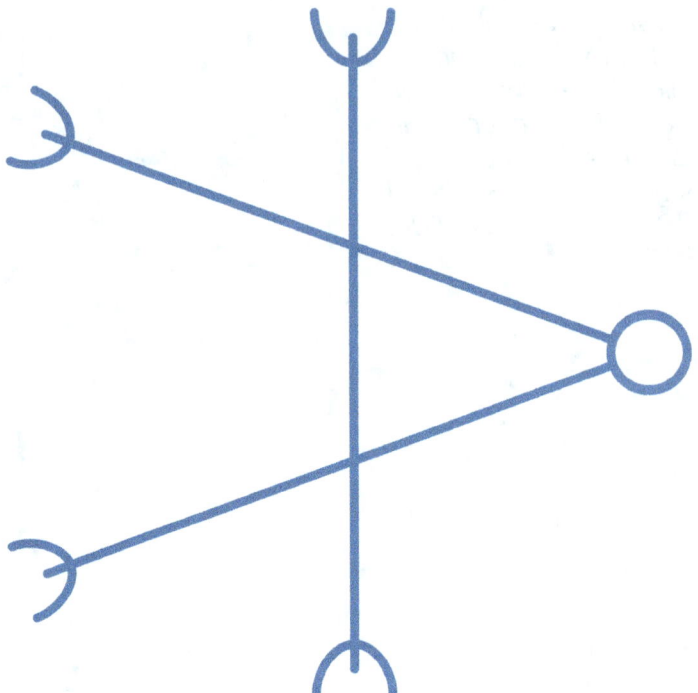

Galdrastafir   11. Legal

Máladeilan, Máldeyfa
(To Win in Court)
LBS 4375 8vo 0001r 02

There are several variations of this stave, the two most common of which are included here.

Inscribe on lignite (jet stone) and colour with blood from your nasal septum, then wear it on your chest. But if you think that you will lose the case, wear a second one on your back, and you will win the case whether it is right or wrong.

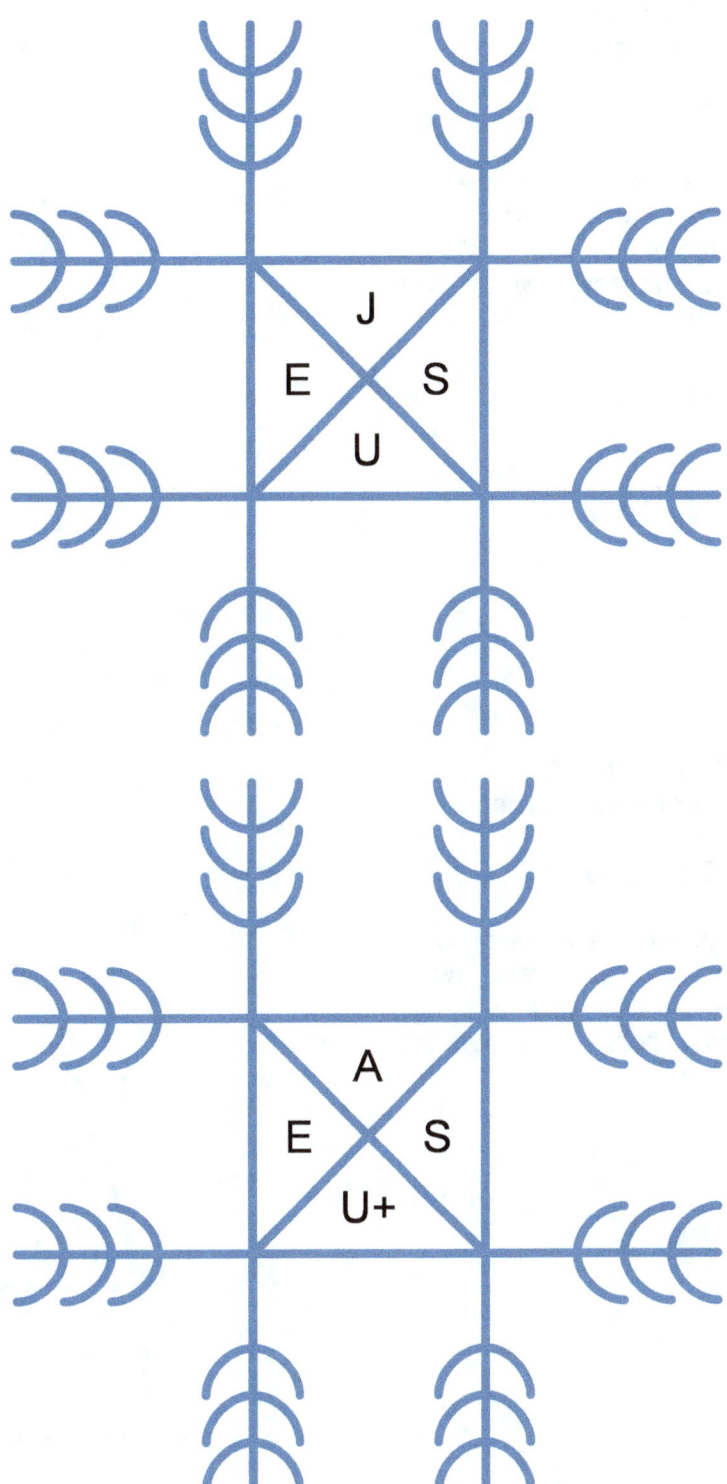

Stafur Til Málfylgju 1
(Stave For Support In Legal Cases 1)
LBS 4375 8vo 0002r 01

If you wish to have the support of others in legal cases, wear this stave inside your clothing, and most people will support your case.

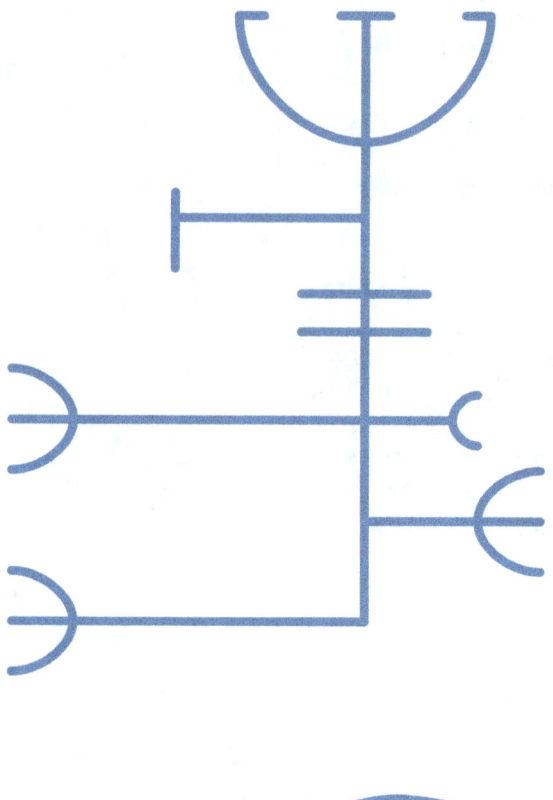

Stafur Til Málfylgju 2
(Stave For Support In Legal Cases 2)
LBS 4375 8vo 0002r 02

If you wish to have the support of others in legal cases, wear this stave inside your clothing, and most people will support your case.

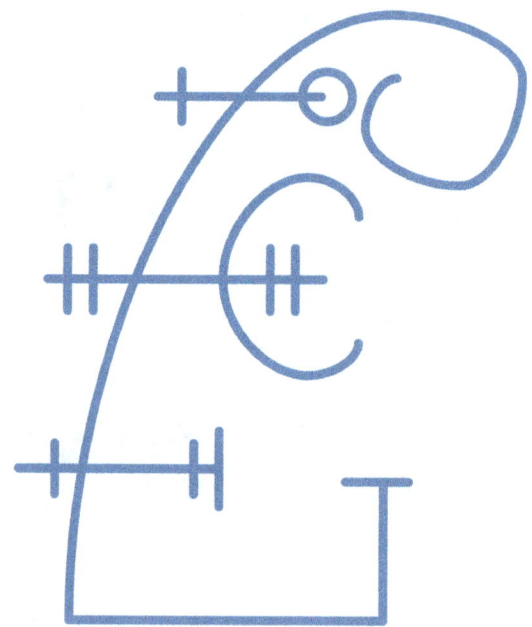

12. Influencing Behaviour

Berreininn, Þagnarstafur
(Bare Stallion, Stave Of Silence)
LBS 4375 8vo 0006r 02

To make someone keep a secret, inscribe this stave on cheese or bread and give it to them to eat.

Fjárspekjustafur
(Stave To Calm Sheep)
LBS 4375 8vo 0001r 03

When the sun rises, take juniper and willow that grows facing the east and carve this stave on it, and let the sheep walk over it in the summers and under it in the winters.

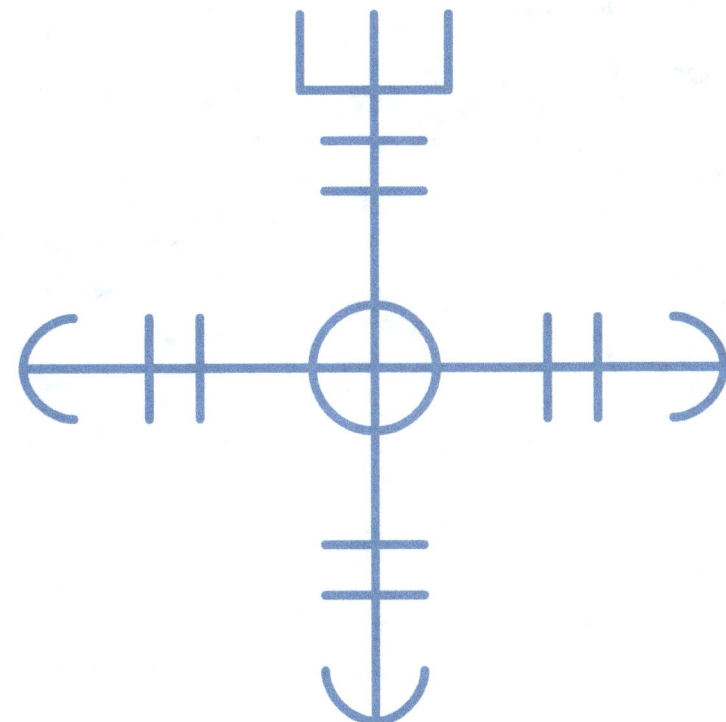

Galdrastafir 12 Influencing Behaviour

Lygastafur 1
(Lying Stave 1)
LBS 2917a 4to 0016v 01
LBS 4627 8vo 0019v 01

If you want to make someone tell a lie, inscribe this stave on leather and place them under their head.

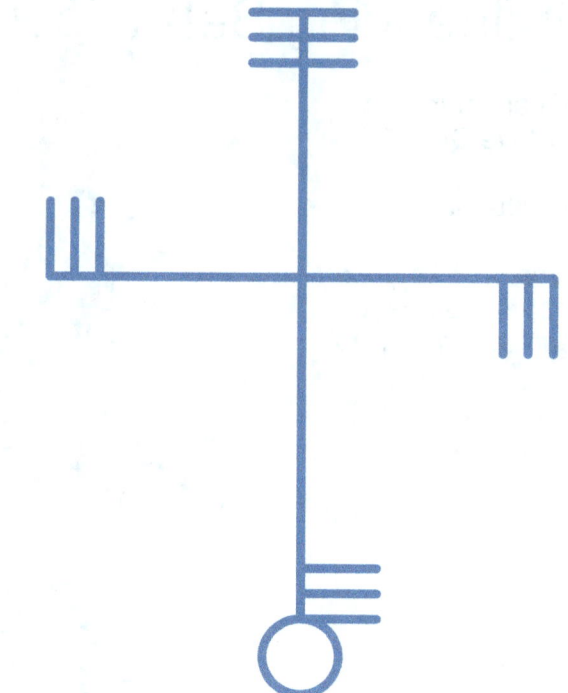

Lygastafur 2
(Lying Stave 2)
LBS 2917a 4to 0016v 02
LBS 4627 8vo 0019v 03

If you want to make someone tell a lie, inscribe this stave on leather and place them under their head.

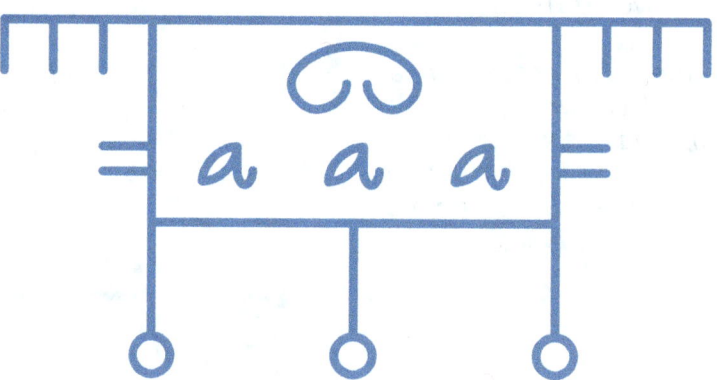

Lygastafur 3
(Lying Stave 3)

If you want to make someone tell a lie, inscribe this stave on leather and place them under their head.

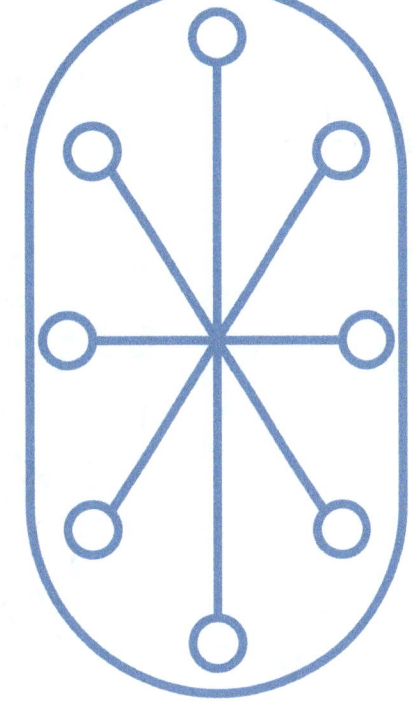

Missýningastafurinn Óðinn
(Delusion Stave of Odin)

This stave may be used at will.

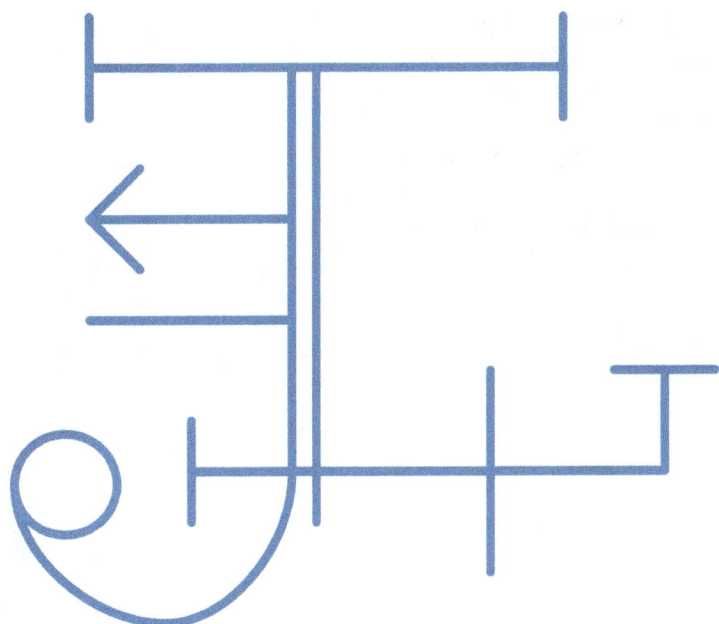

Stafur Til Að Láta Mann Stela (Stave To Make Someone Steal)

If you want to make someone steal, put this stave in his food.

The Silencer

If you don't want someone to talk about you, take this stave and visualise it infusing the person's entire being. He or she will not be able to reveal anything. Also have this stave at your breast for as long as you require discretion.

Galdur Til Að Stilla Alla Reiði
(To Calm Anger)
ATA Amb 2 F 16-26

To still all kinds of wrath make this stave on your forehead with your left index finger, and say 'It is the helm of awe that I bear between my eyes wrath runs away, strife is stemmed'.

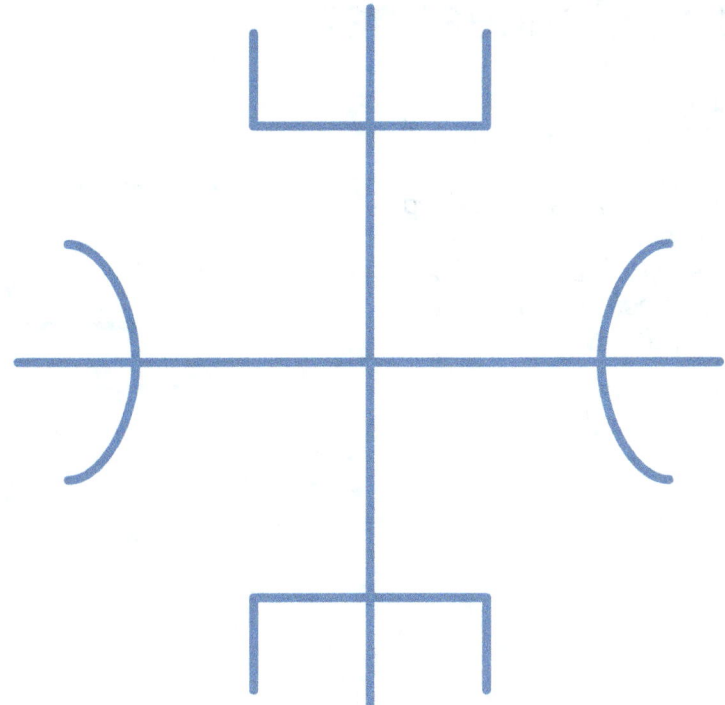

To Put Someone In A Bad Mood

Carve this sign on lead and stick it in the person's clothes at the small of the back.

13. Concealment

Concealment
LBS 2413 8vo 0021r 04

If you want to hide something so it will not be found, carve this stave with your eating knife and the object in question will not be found.

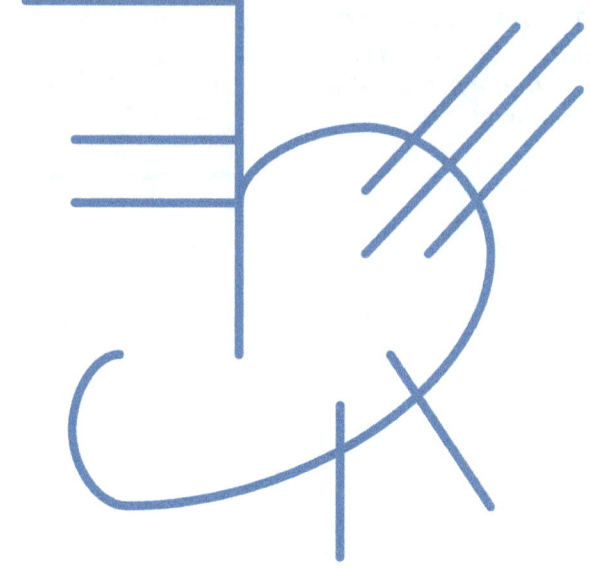

Hulinshjálmur
(Helm Of Concealment)
LBS 4375 8vo 0011v 01
LBS 4375 8vo 0020v 01

Inscribe the stave with magnetised steel on lignite (jet stone). The stave will then conceal you whenever you wish.

Galdrastafir — 13. Concealment

Hulinshringir
(Rings Of Concealment)
LBS 4375 8vo 0005r 02

These rings are to be carved in oak and coloured with blood from the little toe of the left foot, the little finger of the right hand, and the right breast, and kept hidden in your right hand. No one will be able to see you.

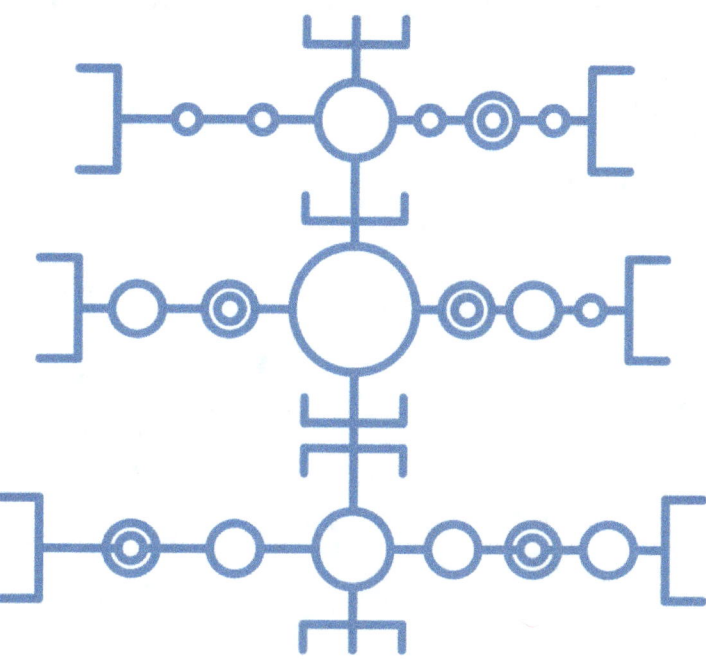

14. Creating Fear in Enemies

Ægishjálmur 1
(Helm of Awe 1)

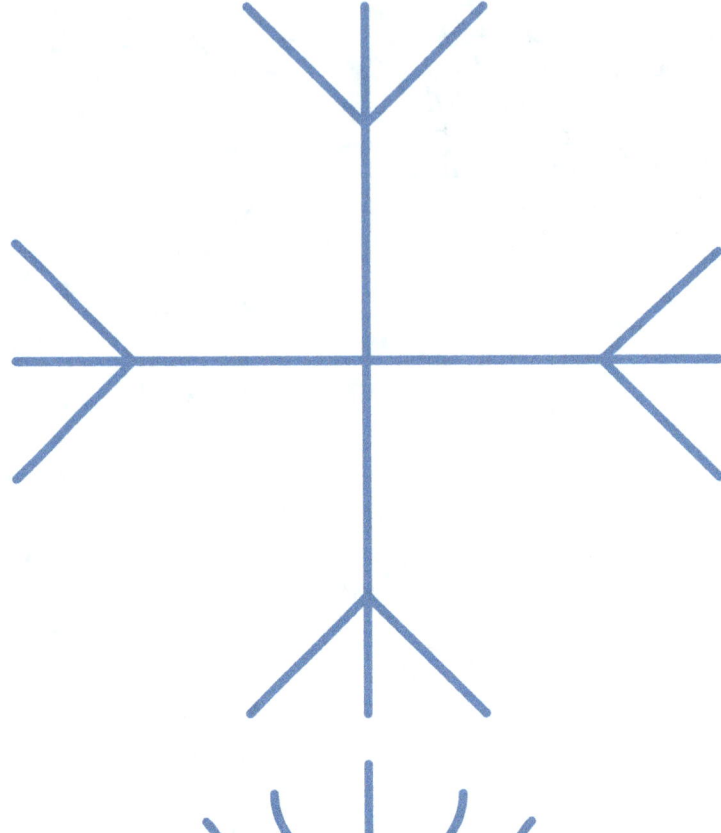

Ægishjálmur 2
(Helm of Awe 2)

Galdrastafir   *14. Creating Fear in Enemies*

Ægishjálmur Hinn Gamli
(Helm of Awe the Elder)
LBS 143 8vo 0011r 01
LBS 2917a 4to 0037v 01
LBS 4375 8vo 0001v 01

To be inscribed on lead, and the lead image pressed into one's forehead between the eyebrows saying 'I bear the helm of terror between my brows!'. Anyone who bears this image against his enemies is guaranteed victory. The Helm of Terror is also trusty protection against the wrath of powerful men saying 'I wash my enemies' hatred off me, the pillage and wrath of wealth men'. This stave is extremely effective.

Galdrastafir   14. Creating Fear in Enemies

Ægisskjöldur Hinn Mikli
(Greater Shield Of Terror)
LBS 4375 8vo 0013r 01

This stave is to be drawn on black paper with bile, and then placed in the nest of a brooding raven. It is to be left there until the raven has hatched its eggs. Then take the paper, and it will be of great use to you. Even if a hundred men were your enemies, and they attacked you and wanted to kill you, this stave would save you easily. If you hold it up before you when facing your enemies, it will appear to them as innumerable black dragons, and that you are preparing to set them loose.

Skelkunarstafur,
Óttastafur
(Fear Stave)
IB 383 4to 0024r 04
LBS 2917a 4to 0011r 02
LBS 4627 8vo 9999r-RB 02

Carve this into an oak staff or small oak plate and throw it at the feet of your foe to frighten him. The stave should be carved with a steel knife.

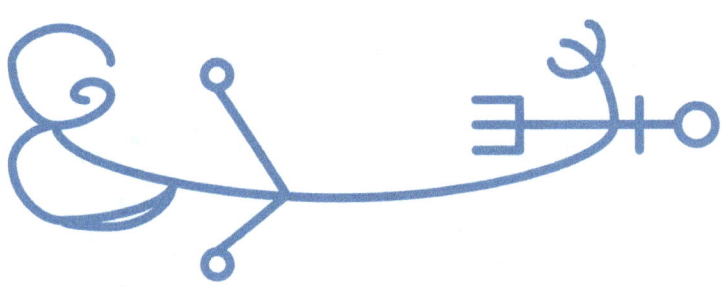

Hræðigaldur
To Cause Fear In An Enemy
ATA Amb 2 F 16-26

If you want your foe to be afraid of you whenever he sees you, then carve these staves on an oak branch and wear it in the middle of your breast--and see to it that you see him before he sees you.

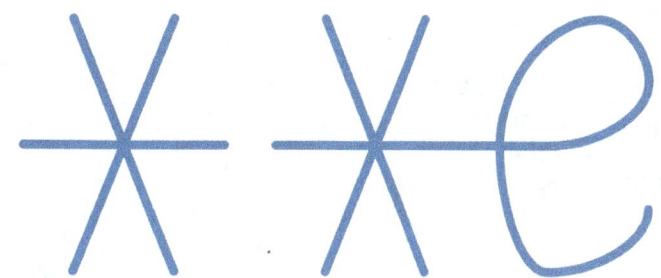

Árásargaldur
(To Cause Fear In Your Enemies)

If you want your enemies to fear you, always carry this stave under your left arm.

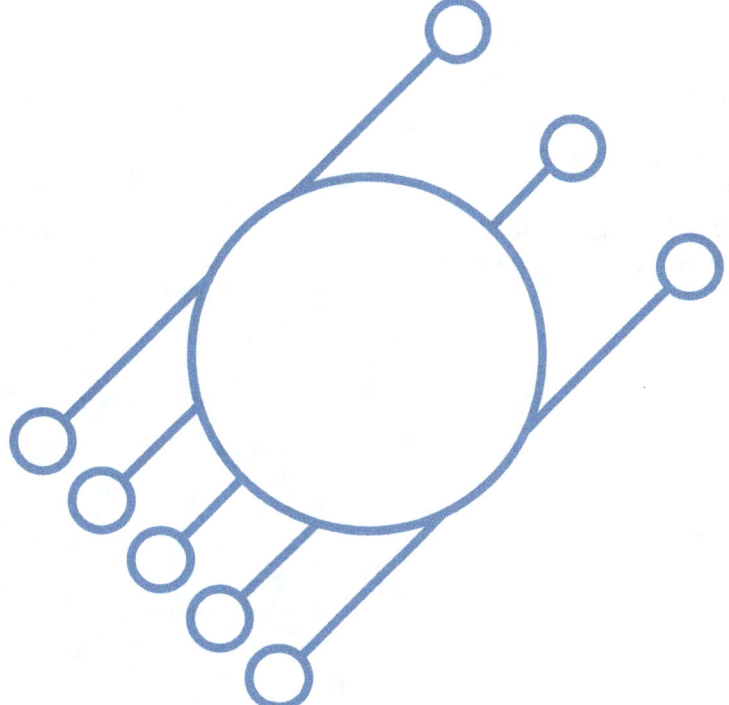

15. Against Enemies

Dreprún
(Killing Rune)
IB 383 4to 0024v 01
LBS 2917a 4to 0011v 01
LBS 4627 8vo 0021v 01

If you want your foe to lose his livestock and possessions, then lay this sign in the hoofprint of his horse.

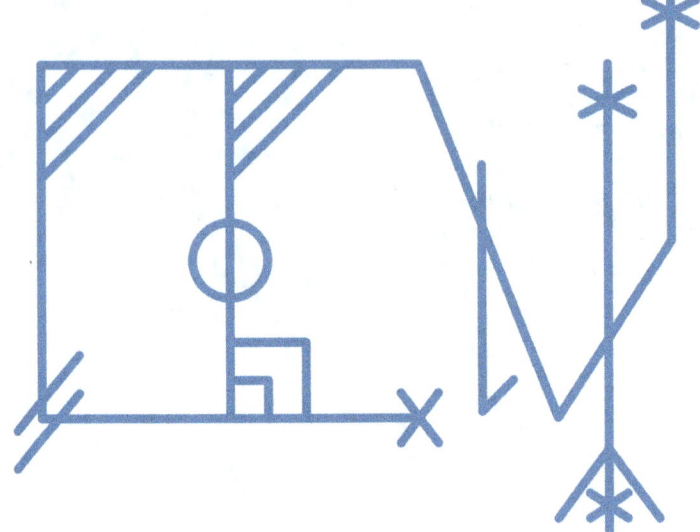

Glettustafur
(Prank Stave)
LBS 2917a 4to 0016r 01

If you wish to play a prank on your enemy, cast this stave at his feet.

Hestafestustafir
(Horse-Fastening Staves)

To make a person become stuck to his horse, inscribe one of these staves in each saddle flap.

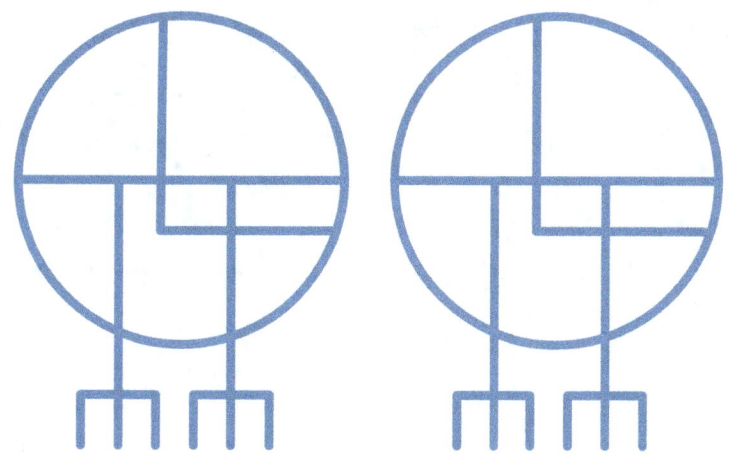

Hringhjálmur
(Ring Helm Or Tide-Mouse Stave)
LBS 4375 8vo 0012v 01

A tide-mouse is a creature summoned by witches to grant people good luck, but eventually their souls are taken and returned to the witch.

Inscribe this stave on catskin from a female stray black cat with a raven's feather in blood, and attach it to the net in which the tide-mouse is to be captured.

Galdrastafir   *15. Against Enemies*

Stafur Mót Óvin Þínum
(Stave Against Your Enemy)
LBS 4375 8vo 0001v 03

If your enemy disputes with you, carry this stave in your left hand.

16. Miscellaneous

Brýnslustafir
(Grinding Staves)
IB 383 4to 0023v 01
LBS 2917a 4to 0009v 02
LBS 4627 8vo 0020r 01]

Carve the upper sign on your whetstone, the other one below, then lay a bit of grass over it, then whet under the sun and don't look at the edge.

Lásabrjotur
(Lock Breaker)
IB 383 4to 0024v 02
LBS 2917a 4to 0012r 01
LBS 4627 8vo 0022r 02

Lay this sign on the lock and blow into it.

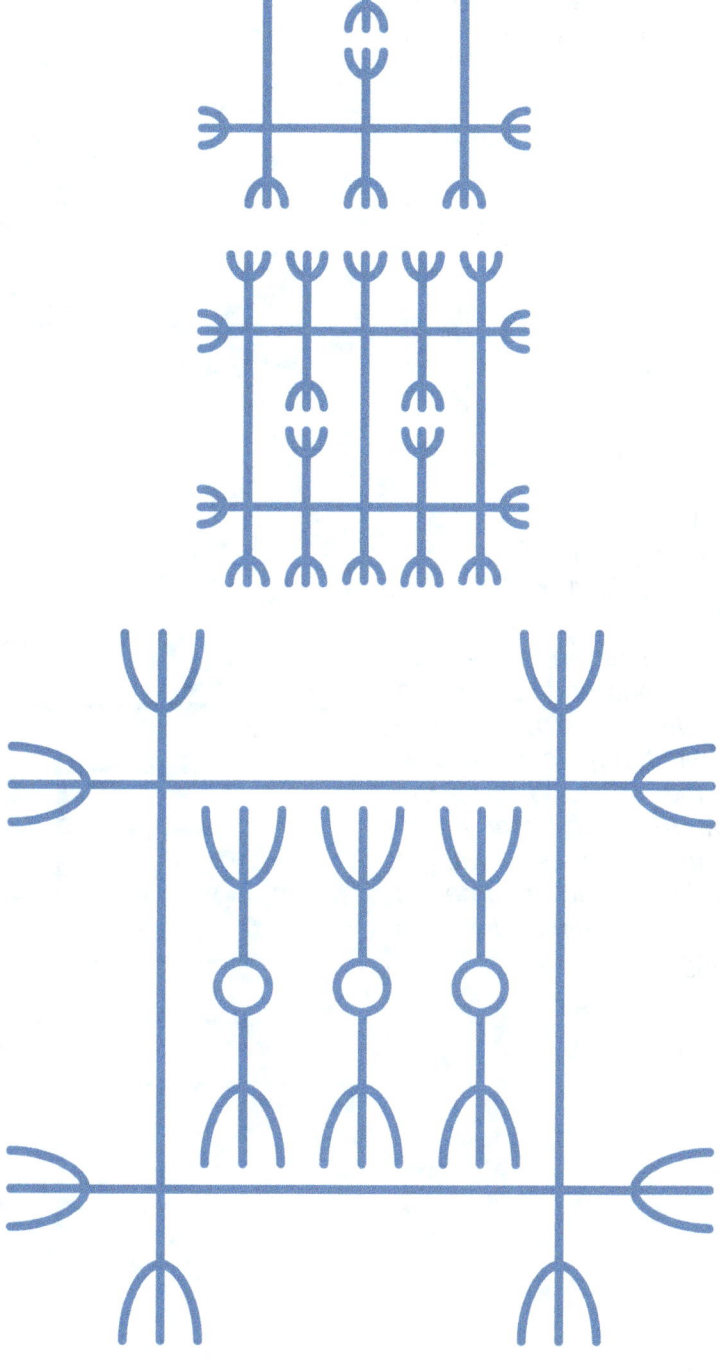

Galdrastafir   16. Miscellaneous

Lásastafur
(Lock Stave)

If you want to open something without a key, place this stave against the lock, blow on it and speak these words: 'May all the trolls take the bolt and tug it, may the devil crack it'.

Vindgapi Meiri
(Greater Blusterer)
LBS 4375 8vo 0011r 01

This is to be cut on the head of a ling (long-bodied edible marine fish), coloured with blood and hung up on a pole where the sea and the land meet at the high-water mark, and the points without semicircles should be turned in the direction whence the wind is coming.

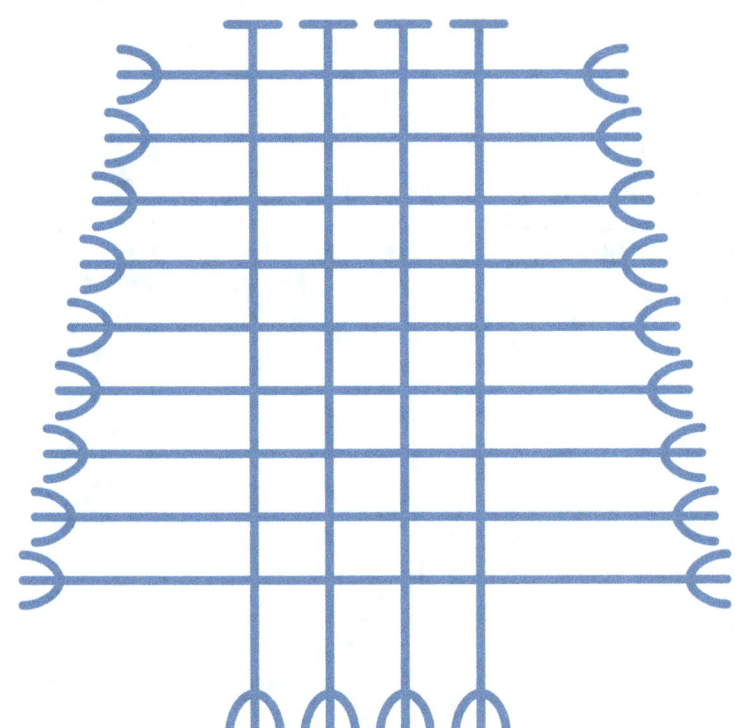

85

Galdrastafir   *16. Miscellaneous*

Vindgapi Minni
(Lesser Blusterer)
LBS 4375 8vo 0011r 02

This is to be cut on the head of a ling (long-bodied edible marine fish), coloured with blood and hung up on a pole where the sea and the land meet at the high-water mark, and the points without semicircles should be turned in the direction whence the wind is coming.

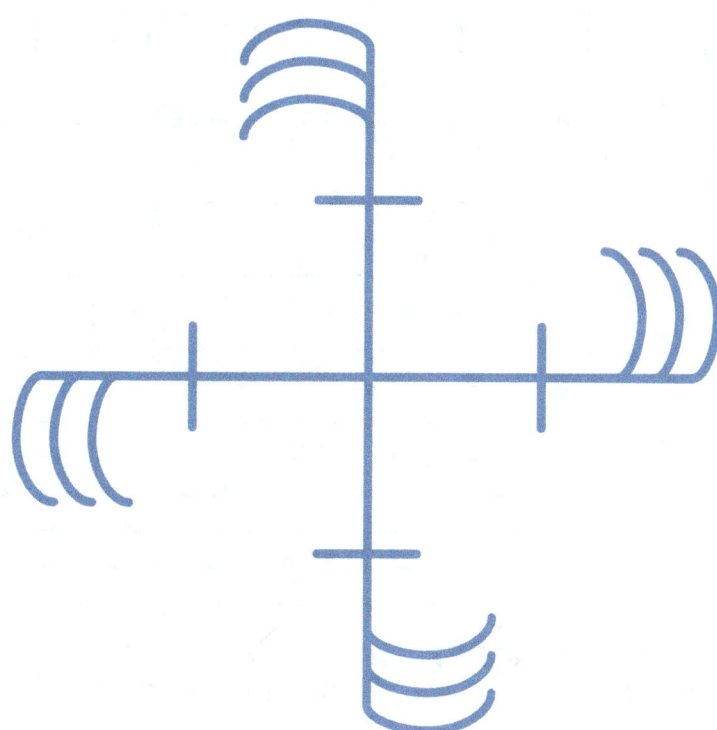

17. The Influence of Christianity

The name 'Rotas Cross' is from the magic table called the 'Sator Square' or 'Rotas Square' which contains a series of 5 letter words in Latin.

S	A	T	O	R
A	R	E	P	O
T	E	N	E	T
O	P	E	R	A
R	O	T	A	S

R	O	T	A	S
O	P	E	R	A
T	E	N	E	T
A	R	E	P	O
S	A	T	O	R

SATOR = The sower, AREPO = (A name), TENET = Holds, OPERA = Work, ROTAS = Turning. Roughly translated this could be said to mean 'The farmer Arepo holds the work of turning the plough'.

The letters when rearranged are also an anagram of 'Pater Noster', the first two words of the Lord's Prayer in Latin.

				P				
				A				
				T				
		A		E		O		
				R				
P	A	T	E	R	N	O	S	T	E	R
				O				
		O		S		A		
				T				
				E				
				R				

Rotas crosses have a talismanic protective quality. The more that are used, the more effective they are.

Galdrastafir   *17. The Influence of Christianity*

Rotaskross 01
(Rotas Cross 01)

Rotaskross 02
(Rotas Cross 02)

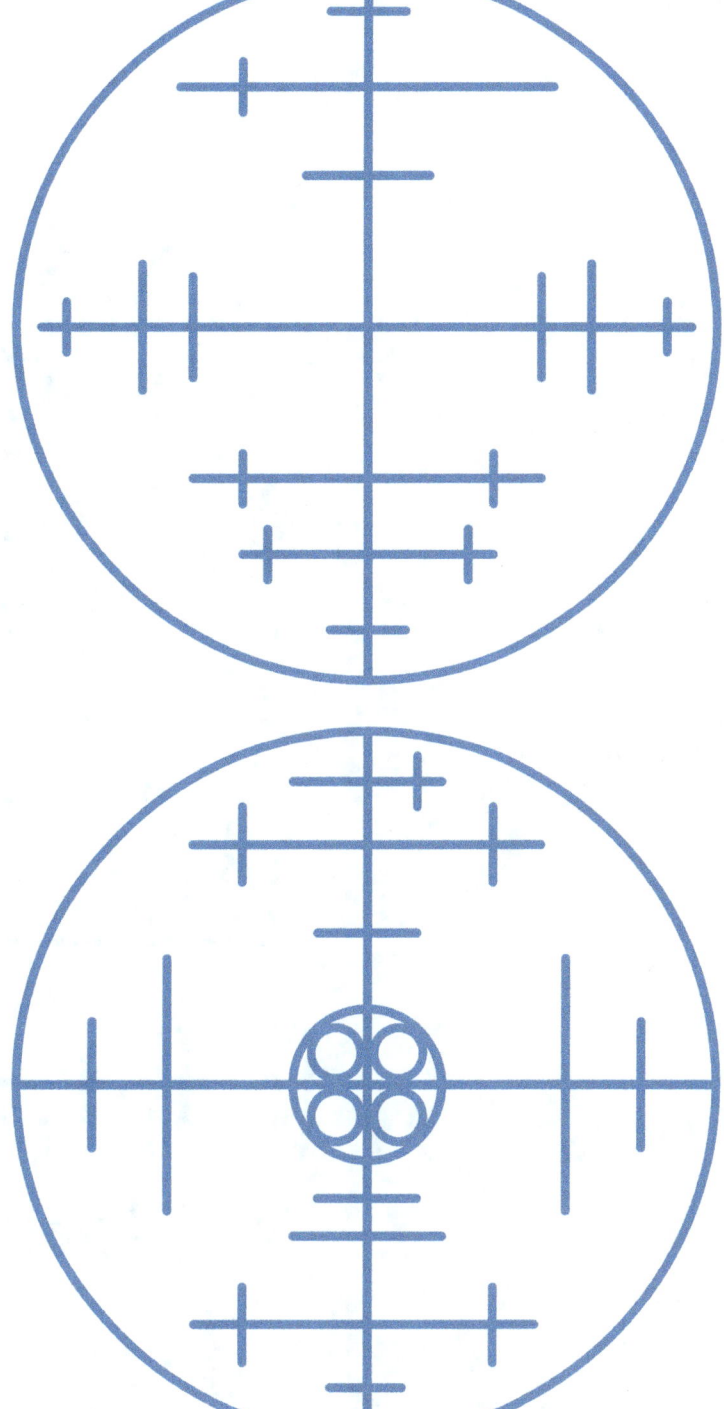

Galdrastafir *17. The Influence of Christianity*

Rotaskross 03
(Rotas Cross 03)

Rotaskross 04
(Rotas Cross 04)

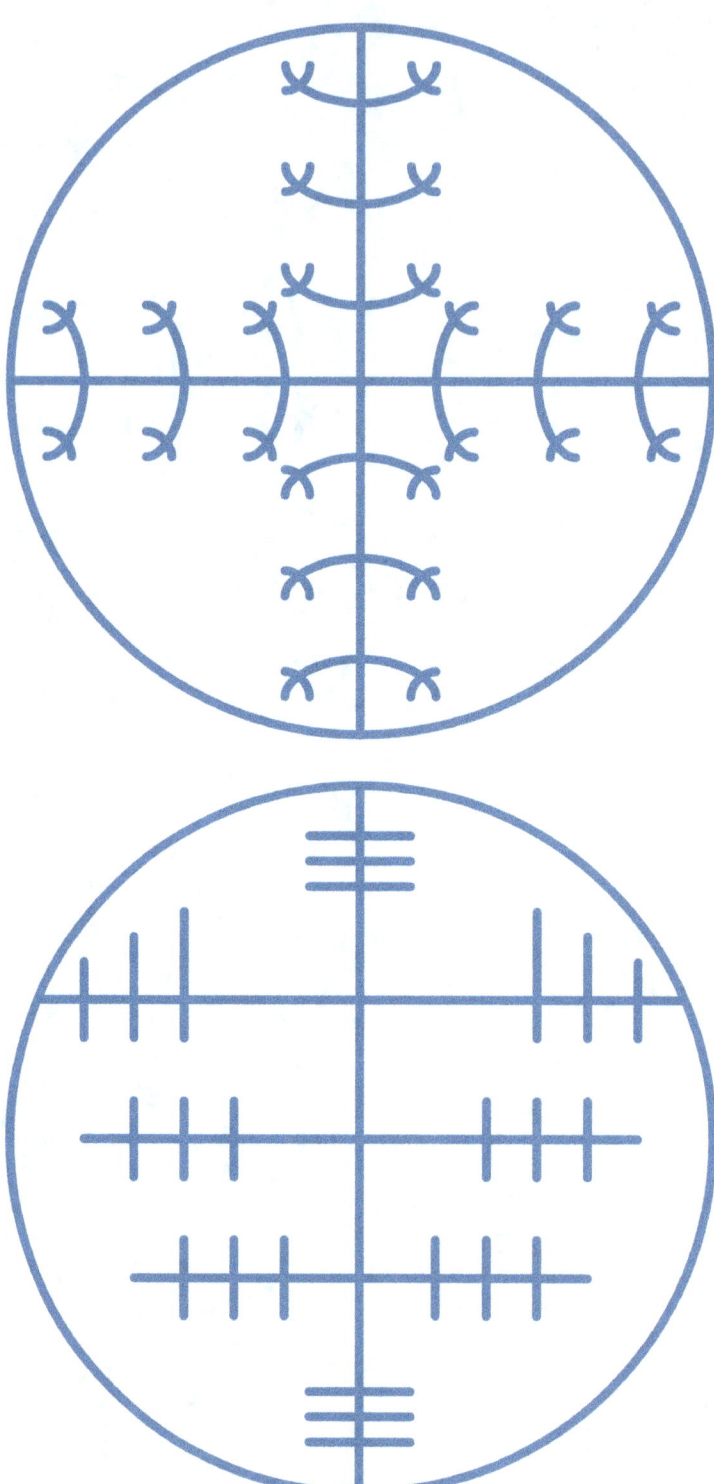

Rotaskross 05
(Rotas Cross 05)

Rotaskross 06
(Rotas Cross 06)

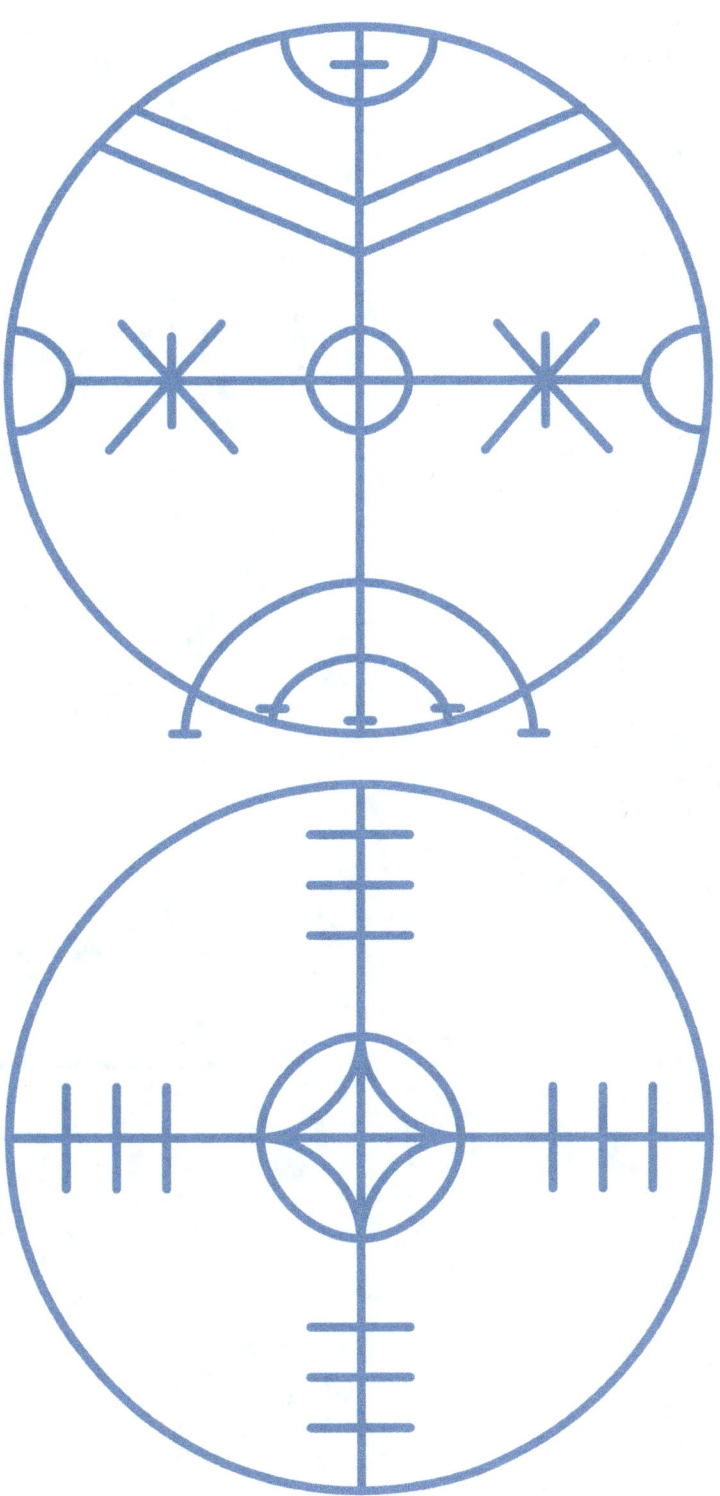

Galdrastafir   17. The Influence of Christianity

Rotaskross 07
(Rotas Cross 07)

Rotaskross 08
(Rotas Cross 08)

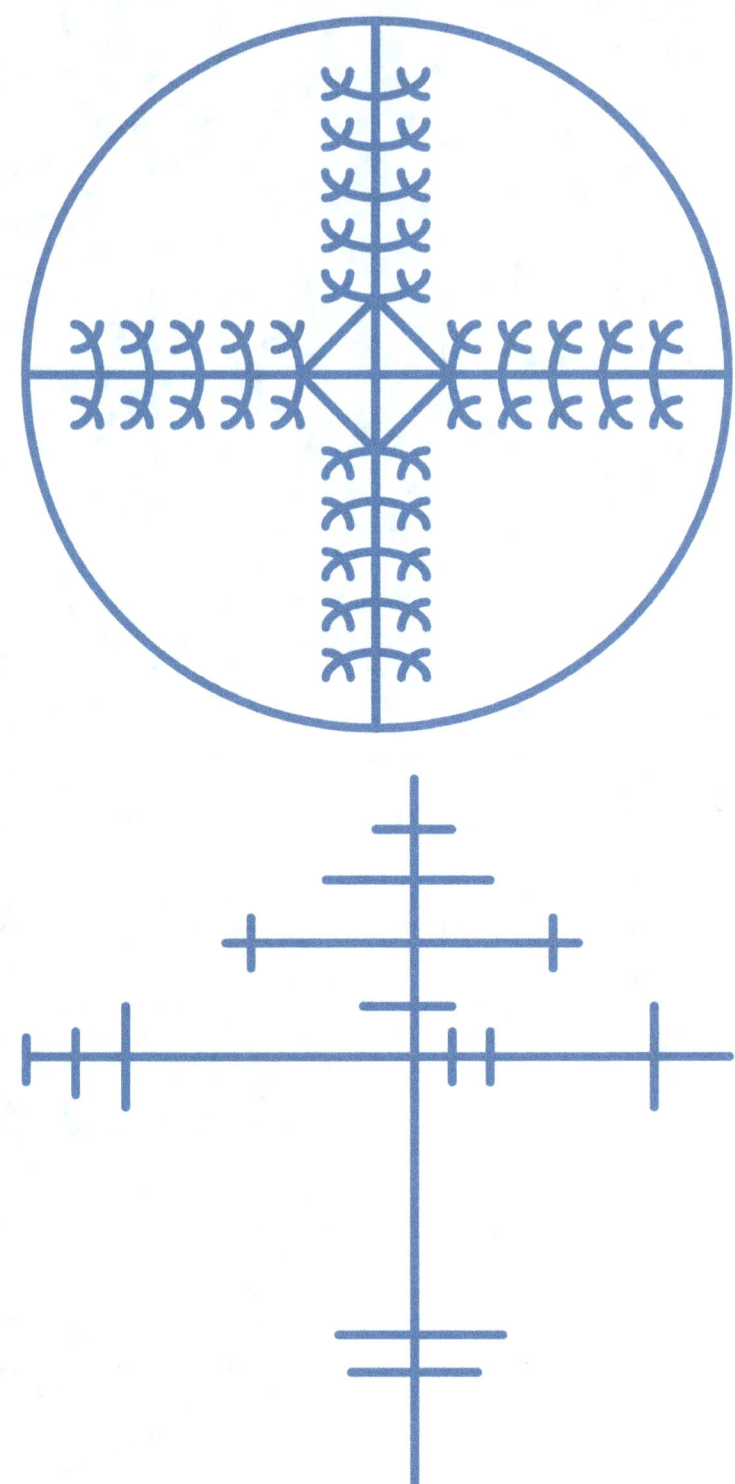

Galdrastafir — *17. The Influence of Christianity*

Rotaskross 09
(Rotas Cross 09)
LBS 977 4to 0034r 04
LBS 4375 8vo 0001v 02
LBS 4375 8vo 0003v 02

Rotaskross 10
(Rotas Cross 10)
LBS 2917a 4to 0033r 01

**Rotaskross Eiriks Jarls
(Lesser Rotas Cross Of Earl Eirikur)**

**Rotaskross Olafs Konungs
(Rotas Cross Of The King Olafur)
IB 383 4to 0026r 02**

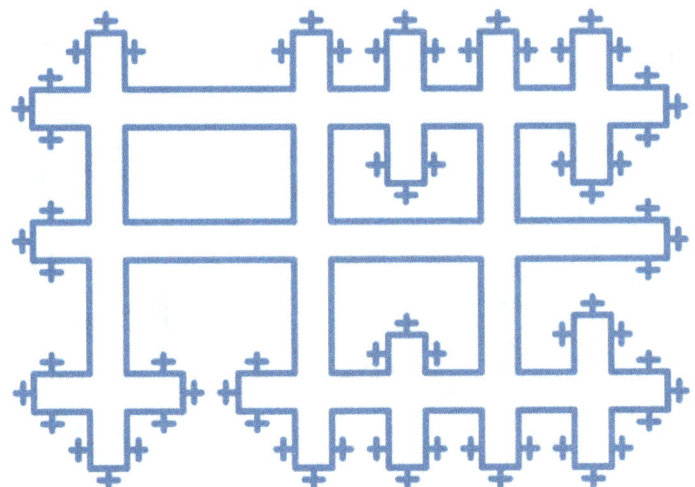

Galdrastafir   *17. The Influence of Christianity*

Rotaskross Stefnis
(Stefnir's Rotas Cross)

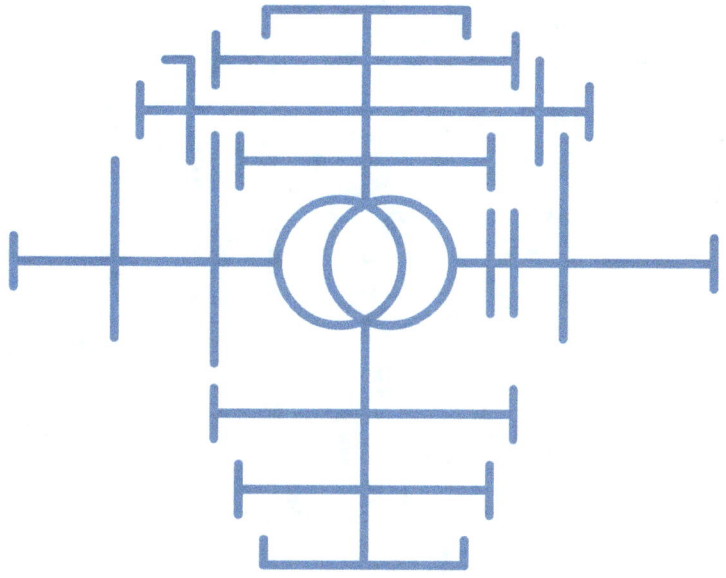

Rothukross
(Crucifix)
IB 383 4to 0026r 01
LBS 2917a 4to 0014v 01

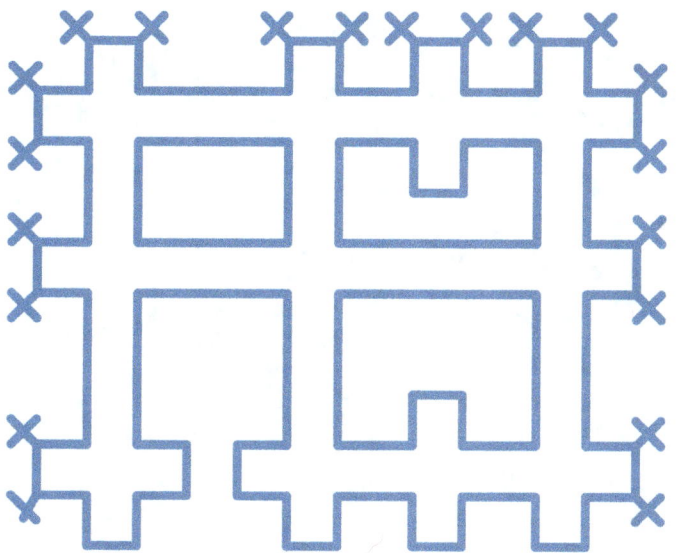

www.ingramcontent.com/pod-product-compliance
Lightning Source LLC
Chambersburg PA
CBHW051420070526
44584CB00023B/3505